FLICKERING SHADOWS

HOW PULPDOM'S MASTER OF DARKNESS BRIGHTENED THE SILVER SCREEN

ED HULSE

MURANIA PRESS

DOVER, NEW JERSEY

Copyright © 2016 by Murania Press

The Shadow copyright © 2016 Advance Magazine Publishers Inc. d/b/a Condé Nast. "The Shadow," "The Shadow face design," and the phrase "Who knows what evil lurks in the hearts of men?" are registered trademarks of Advance Magazine Publishers Inc. d/b/a Condé Nast. The phrases "The Shadow knows" and "The weed of crime bears bitter fruit" are trademarks owned by Advance Magazine Publishers Inc. d/b/a Condé Nast.

Shadow Magazine covers reprinted herein copyright © 2016 Advance Magazine Publishers Inc. d/b/a Condé Nast.

Portions of this book originally appeared in different form in several volumes of Shadow pulp reprints published by Sanctum Books of San Antonio, Texas.

Stills, posters, lobby cards, and frame captures from Universal's Shadow featurettes are copyright © 2016 by NBCUniversal, a Comcast Company. Stills, posters, lobby cards, and frame captures from Columbia's Shadow serial are copyright © 2016 by Sony Pictures Entertainment Motion Picture Group.

ISBN-13: 978-1537559391
ISBN-10: 1537559397

All rights reserved. No part of this publication may be reproduced, stored in a retrieval system, or transmitted in any form by all means—electronic, mechanical, photocopying, audio recording, or otherwise—without the written permission of the copyright holder.

Murania Press
Dover, New Jersey
muraniapress.com
muraniapress@yahoo.com

Book Design and Layout: Ed Hulse

Printed in the United States of America

REVISED AND CORRECTED SECOND EDITION

10 9 8 7 6 5 4 3 2

INTRODUCTION

THIS REVISED SECOND EDITION replaces the 2016 first printing, correcting some stylistic and typographic errors that escaped my eagle eyes during proofreading. I've also taken the opportunity of replacing a few poorly chosen words here and there. The result is a smoother read that reflects my original intention.

Flickering Shadows has been extremely successful for Murania Press, outselling everything in the line except *The Blood 'n' Thunder Guide to Pulp Fiction* during 2017. Typically, my books get unanimous five-star reviews from Amazon customers, and this one followed in the footsteps of previous releases—with one glaring exception. A miffed purchaser gave this book two stars and headlined his review "The Shadow has the last laugh." He went on to say, "The author does a good deal of research to tell us how bad the Shadow movies were. . . . I only have one question, if these movies were so bad, why are they being talked about 60 years later?"

Truth be told, I was seriously annoyed by his criticism. Rather than debit me for poor writing or faulty research, this buyer gave the book a two-star review essentially because he disagreed with the conclusions I'd reached. But in the months since his notice was filed I've come to realize that he had a valid point.

It's true that I'm pretty tough on the various Shadow films, and I can understand why a reader might reasonably arrive at the conclusion that I'm not really a fan of the character. This couldn't be further from the truth; my own fascination with The Shadow dates back to a 1962 television screening of *The Shadow Returns*, one of the 1946 Monogram features starring Kane Richmond. The Master of Darkness hooked me as a nine-year-old boy, and more than a half century later he's still one of my favorite fictional heroes.

Yet the truth is inescapable: Hollywood has never done right by The Shadow. Not one of his celluloid incarnations has ever accurately portrayed either the pulp-fiction or radio-drama version of the character. As a critic and a historian I have to call 'em like I see 'em. But that doesn't mean the films aren't worth seeing; if I thought that, I would never have bothered writing this monograph. Please keep that in mind as you wade through the following pages. I guarantee you'll find the effort rewarding. —*Ed Hulse*

The first two *Shadow Magazine* covers sported old paintings commissioned for earlier Street & Smith pulps. Issues three through five had covers painted by Jerome Rozen, whose brother George took over with issue six. This iconic image adorned the August 1, 1933 cover and was also used on advertising and promotional items.

TO A NOT-INSIGNIFICANT NUMBER OF ENTHUSIASTS, the term "pulp fiction" immediately calls to mind the single-character magazines featuring such popular heroes as The Shadow, Doc Savage, and The Spider. This is especially true of baby-boomers who gravitated to pulps from the comic-book world, which remains dominated by superheroes. It should be noted that some aficionados disdain the single-character titles, believing them juvenile and silly, but during the Depression years they gave a much-needed shot of adrenalin to the badly weakened, nearly moribund pulp-publishing industry. Only one of these characters, however, had widespread success in multiple mediums—including motion pictures.

The Shadow was the first pulp hero to get his own magazine. Created in 1930 as the narrator of *Street & Smith's Detective Story Hour*, a weekly radio program, this eerie personage captivated listeners with his ominous asides and sinister chuckles. The character's popularity rapidly surpassed that of the pulp he promoted (the Thursday-night series dramatized yarns from *Detective Story Magazine*), and Street & Smith brass decided to capitalize on it by launching a title devoted to this mysterious crime fighter.

Initially entrusted to *Detective Story* editor Frank Blackwell, *The Shadow, a Detective Magazine* debuted in early 1931 as a quarterly. Freelance journalist and editor Walter B. Gibson was hired to write The Shadow's novel-length adventures under the house name Maxwell Grant. With very little to go on—after all, the character didn't actually participate in the dramatized radio stories—Gibson created a hero with unusual qualities, stitching him together from flimsy patches of story material. At the outset, The Shadow had no other identity. "The Living Shadow," his first story, focused more on Harry Vincent, a suicidal young man rescued by The Shadow and pressed into service as one of his agents in the war on crime. Gibson told the story from Vincent's point of view; at periodic intervals The Shadow materialized as if from thin air to aid his new recruit and apprehend secondary villains. To tie in with the radio Shadow, Gibson explained that the spectral sleuth appeared on weekly broadcasts to transmit coded messages to such agents as might be listening. It seemed like an unnecessarily complicated method by which to relay instructions but provided readers with a connection to the *Detective Story Hour*.

In the second novel, "The Eyes of the Shadow" (July-September 1931), Gibson hinted that his mystery man was millionaire Lamont Cranston, a world traveler and New York clubman. But the third story, "The Shadow Laughs" (October 1931), revealed that the mysterious avenger only impersonated Cranston, whose incessant globetrotting made him an easy

This 1936 issue introduced several of The Shadow's agents, who assisted him in the fight against crime and often acted as what author Walter B. Gibson called "proxy heroes"— in other words, they moved a story's action forward until The Shadow was ready to make his next whirlwind appearance, guns blazing.

man to double. The next several series entries introduced readers to other recently recruited agents, who assisted the Master of Darkness (one of several colorful nicknames Gibson coined) in his war on crime.

Gibson's early efforts reflect the author's nostalgic attraction to dime novels of the Horatio Alger and Nick Carter period. His were not tersely written, realistic crime stories of the *Black Mask* type; they relied on character types and plot conventions straight out of Frank L. Packard's Jimmie Dale yarns, published a generation earlier in Street & Smith's *People's Magazine* and relying on gaslight-era tropes.

Nonetheless, *The Shadow Magazine* (as it was soon retitled) became enormously successful, going from quarterly to monthly almost immediately and becoming a bi-weekly in October 1932. Writing a full-length novel every two weeks would have burned out most writers within a couple years, but Gibson maintained that pace for a full decade, thanks to regular consultations with veteran Street & Smith executive Henry W. Ralston and editor John Nanovic, whose brainstorming helped him come up with ideas. The novels turned out by Gibson between late '32 and early '37 are the ones most diligently collected by Shadow fans. Obviously, some of them are clinkers; Dickens himself could not have maintained Gibson's schedule without writing a few stiffs here and there. By and large, though, given the limitations of Gibson's talent and methodology, the Shadow stories of these years retained the magic that made the character a pop-culture sensation. And make no mistake, he *was* a sensation: Within a few short years *The Shadow Magazine* sold an estimated 300,000 copies per issue, a sales threshold seldom reached by any pulp magazine during the Thirties.

The first novel to show Gibson cooking on all burners was "The Romanoff Jewels" (December 1, 1932), a cynical tale pitting The Shadow against a host of unsympathetic characters operating at cross-purposes. Equally meritorious was "The Grove of Doom" (September 1, 1933), an eerie yarn that stressed atmosphere over action. An isolated grove of copper beeches on Long Island provided an unusual setting for villainous depredations and hid an equally unusual killer. "Fingers of Death" (March 1, 1933) presented a well-formulated story revolving around serial murders—a Gibson plot staple.

The Shadow yarns of this period were intricate, sometimes needlessly so. The author preferred it that way. Walter Gibson's imagination was boundless and his love of stage magic manifested itself in a penchant for misdirection, which he used to good advantage. He also briefly exhibited a fascination for the grotesque, dabbling with bizarre concepts aimed at tantalizing the readers. One early novel, "The Black Master" (March 1, 1932), hinted that The Shadow remained shrouded in darkness because he had no face. Another excellent story, "The Shadow's Shadow" (February 1, 1933), matched the cloaked crime fighter against an adversary he had encountered previously, as a flying spy during the Great War.

Gibson's prose was anything but vivid. He wrote stilted dialogue, relied too much on passive verb constructions, and padded action sequences shamelessly, often taking several thousand words to describe a gunfight that lasted 30 seconds in real time. He resorted to ending chapters with lengthy "teasers" alluding to events that would soon transpire. Yet the magazine's readers hung on his every word. The radio Shadow had a larger audience, but his pulp incarnation developed an almost fanatically loyal following.

Many Shadow buffs believe the magazine's peak period began in early 1934, specifically with "Gray Fist" (February 15, 1934), an unusually actionful tale distinguished by a master criminal's disruption of The Shadow's organization. Other notable series installments from this year included "The Green Box" (March 15), which sported a classic Shadow cover

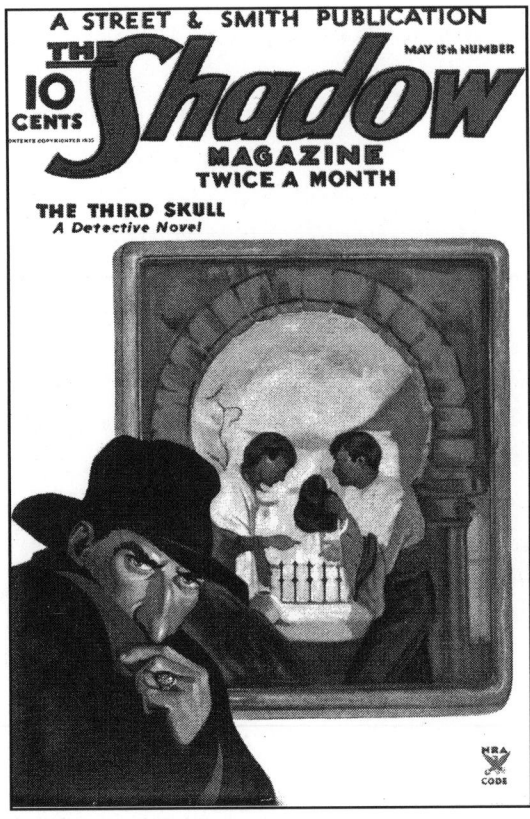

"The Third Skull" (1935) was one of the finest early Shadow novels, although this beautifully executed cover by George Rozen gave away the solution to the mystery: that the long-sought-after third skull was an optical illusion in a painting!

portrait and introduced Hawkeye, an underworld spy who became one of the chief agents; "The Cobra" (April 1), with its cleverly disguised villain; and "The Crime Master" (August 1), featuring a super-genius who conducted his criminal campaign like a chess game.

In my view *The Shadow Magazine* reached its zenith in 1935, a year that saw a high concentration of above-average novels, two of which are strong contenders for the series' best. Many of today's fans believe, as Gibson himself did, that "Zemba" (December 1) is the finest Shadow adventure. It took place largely in Paris, where The Shadow matched wits with enigmatic master spy Gaspard Zemba. My personal favorite is "Lingo" (April 1), which may well be the *quintessential* Shadow adventure. It was well plotted, unfolded on The Shadow's home turf of New York, made good use of his agents, boasted one of the series' best action climaxes, and hinged on a deception Gibson carried off masterfully.

Other 1935 jewels included "Bells of Doom" (March 15), a spooky, cleverly developed mystery; "The Third Skull" (May 15), featuring an ingenious puzzle to which George Rozen's skillfully executed cover painting

This early publicity photo for the Shadow radio program shows Frank Readick, best of the role's early interpreters, in snap-brim fedora, mask, and high-collared cloak, which became his standard uniform. Readick wore this same outfit in his brief stint as the movies' first Shadow.

supplied the crucial piece; "The Fate Joss" (July 1), a fast-moving Chinatown yarn that introduced Dr. Roy Tam, who would become a trusted agent; and "The Python" (November 15), a non-formula series entry that began with The Shadow, in his Cranston guise, already unconscious and in the hands of ruthless enemies.

No less than four 1936 novels appeared on a Top Ten list compiled from a poll of readers and printed in the magazine's letter column the following year. "The Voodoo Master" (March 1) sported a memorable cover depicting The Shadow clad in red to maintain relative invisibility in a chamber draped with cloth of the same hue. It was the first of three tales setting the Master of Darkness against Dr. Rodil Mocquino, a ruthless hypnotist and devotee of the Black Arts who commanded an army of zombies. "City of Doom" (May 15) and "Voodoo Trail" (June 1, 1938) were worthy sequels. "The Gray Ghost" (May 1), a fast-action mystery featuring a spectral nemesis, took the Number One spot in the aforementioned Top Ten list, although it doesn't seem particularly impressive today, perhaps because its "surprise" ending depends on a hokey gimmick that was old even

This promotional portrait of Frank Readick in character was distributed during the early Thirties, before the radio show devoted itself to recounting The Shadow's own adventures. "Blue Coal" was the unique product of the Delaware, Lackawanna, and Western Coal Company, which sponsored *Detective Story Hour* and, later, *The Shadow*. Blue Coal premiums featuring the Master of Darkness were plentiful and unbiquitous; they can still be found in ample supply today on the internet auction site eBay and from antique dealers who specialize in such memorabilia.

in 1936. "The Golden Masks" (September 1), another breathlessly paced yarn, fell back on the oft-used but still effective device of a bizarrely costumed criminal cadre.

Two other 1936 entries were exceptionally strong. "The Salamanders" (April 1), an action-packed romp about arsonists, moved at an unusually rapid pace. One of Rozen's very best covers, showing The Shadow hoisting a gigantic, severed head, adorned "The Crime Oracle" (June 1), another inventive tale that showcased Gibson's love of illusion and stagecraft.

"Partners of Peril" (November 1, 1936) featured a dynamic, iconic George Rozen painting that showed The Shadow in vignette, twin automatics blazing and sable cloak fluttering. The so-so story inside was the first of 27 Shadow exploits written by Theodore Tinsley under the Maxwell Grant byline normally used by Gibson alone.

Nineteen Thirty-Seven was a transitional year for *The Shadow Magazine*. By this time Walter Gibson had penned over a hundred novels featuring the same principal character and supporting cast, and he began repeating himself with alarming frequency. Among the first dozen Shadow yarns to see print that year only two were winners, "The Shadow's Rival" (June 15) and "Crime, Insured" (July 1). The latter employed a unique plot gimmick: The villain, after investing considerable time in spying on The Shadow and his agents, became confident enough in his ability to anticipate their moves that he offered insurance against their interference to criminals plotting assorted depredations. Gibson's departure from formula paid off handsomely with this one.

With the consent and assistance of editor Nanovic, Gibson upended the series with "The Shadow Unmasks" (August 1, 1937), a misfire that signaled the beginning of the magazine's decline. For the most part a mundane story, "Unmasks" was memorable only for revealing to readers that their hero was in reality Kent Allard, a famous aviator presumed lost after his airplane crashed somewhere in the jungles of Guatemala. Dropping out of sight, he spent several years undercover, living with Xinca Indians while amassing great wealth and preparing for a lengthy war on crime. Returning to the United States, he set up shop in New York and began recruiting agents—a process to which readers had been introduced at the beginning of the very first novel, "The Living Shadow" (April 1931), when the black-cloaked figure saved Harry Vincent from suicide.

Following the publication in late 1937 of two outstanding entries—Tinsley's railroad mystery "The Pooltex Tangle" (October 1) and Gibson's Chinatown opus "Teeth of the Dragon" (November 15)—the magazine continued its slow slide to mediocrity. The late Thirties issues yielded a plethora of acceptably entertaining novels but few memorable ones. One bright spot of this period was the hiring of Edd Cartier to produce black-and-white interior illustrations. Cartier, who began selling artwork to Street & Smith in 1936, initially shared *Shadow Magazine* chores with Tom Lovell, whose style he attempted to emulate for several months. After Lovell quit the pulp in late 1937, Cartier became the series' primary illustrator, a job he held until the spring of 1940, when he was replaced by Earl Mayan, who later that year relinquished the assignment to Paul Orban.

Among the most memorable entries from this period are "The Fifth Napoleon" (February 1, 1938), an especially intricate, above-average Tinsley; "The Golden Vulture" (July 15, 1938), Gibson's rewrite of a Shadow novel submitted in 1932 by *Doc Savage* writer Lester Dent; "Shadow Over Alcatraz" (December 1, 1938); "Death's Harlequin" (May 1, 1939); and "The Masked Lady" (October 15, 1939). The 1938-39 Shadow adventures included some splashes of sex, which Tinsley deftly inserted. Gibson, who rarely limned female characters credibly, and often did without them altogether in his stories, seemed ill at ease writing mildly spicy scenes but did so dutifully, presumably by editorial request.

Two sub-series featuring recurring villains deserve special mention. The Shadow's answer to Fu Manchu was Shiwan Khan, a malevolent celestial who figured in four novels: "The Golden Master" (September 15, 1939), "Shiwan Khan Returns" (December 1, 1939), "The Invincible Shiwan Khan" (March 1, 1940), and "Masters of Death" (May 15, 1940). The quartet's final story, with its occult phenomena and Shadow-Shiwan duel to the death, was by far the best.

Theodore Tinsley got into the act with Benedict Stark, a diminutive, grotesquely shaped tycoon whose warped mind concocted criminal schemes for the sheer joy of doing evil. Sadistic and shocking, the Stark stories were strikingly different than the average Shadows cranked out by Gibson. Tinsley even went so far in the second one, "The Murder Genius" (July 1, 1940), as to kill off young lovers introduced in the yarn's early pages. The sub-series began with "The Prince of Evil" (April 15, 1940) and also included "The Man Who Died Twice" (September 15, 1940) and "The Devil's Paymaster" (November 15, 1940).

In 1937 The Shadow, after a two-year absence from the nation's airwaves, returned in a eponymous weekly program produced by the same advertising agency that had masterminded the *Detective Story Hour*. This time, the Master of Darkness was hero rather than narrator, figuring

Orson Welles had already acquired a reputation as the theater's "enfant terrible" when he agreed to play The Shadow during the show's 1937-38 season.

prominently in every episode. But he wasn't exactly the same Shadow to whom the pulp-magazine readers had become accustomed. He was called Lamont Cranston, but instead of wearing sable hat and cloak to help him blend into darkness, this Shadow used his ability to cloud men's minds so they couldn't see him—a little trick he picked up in the Orient.

Outfitted with a lovely friend and companion, one Margot Lane, Cranston exploited his friendship with Police Commissioner Ralph Weston to gain proximity to crime scenes. Boy genius Orson Welles initially played The Shadow but in the fall of 1938 was replaced by Bill Johnstone, who proved equally popular in the role. (The original Margot, prolific radio actress Agnes Moorehead, later followed Welles to Hollywood and debuted on the big screen, as he did, in *Citizen Kane*.) The radio show's burgeoning popularity forced Nanovic to acknowledge it by having Gibson incorporate Margot—whose name eventually lost its "t"—into the pulp series. She made her printed-page debut in "The Thunder King" (June 15, 1941).

The early Forties saw a waning of Gibson's ingenuity. In addition to writing two novels a month, he was also scripting stories for Street & Smith's *Shadow Comics* and, increasingly, dumbing down the prose yarns for youthful readers. I can't honestly recommend any 1941-43 novels with the exceptions of "The Money Master" (December 15, 1942) and "Death's Masquerade" (January 15, 1943). The former was a topical tale featuring a ruthless war profiteer, the latter a murder mystery set in New Orleans during Mardi Gras.

By the end of 1943, *The Shadow* was no longer published twice a month, no longer issued in standard pulp size, and no longer edited by John Nanovic. Now a digest-sized monthly (thanks to wartime paper restrictions, which wreaked havoc with the entire industry), the preeminent single-character pulp settled into its most dismal phase. Gibson tailored his stories to reflect the radio show's steadily growing popularity. Margo was very much in evidence, and the role of taxi driver Moe Shrevnitz—called "Shrevvy" on the air—was beefed up in recognition of his prominence on the airwaves. With World War II in full swing, the super-criminals and their henchmen largely went into retirement, leaving The Shadow to solve routine murder cases and tangle with black marketers or the occasional Fifth Columnist.

Few of the digest novels stand out. Among the better ones were "The Freak-Show Murders" (May 1944), "Voodoo Death" (June 1944), and "The Mask of Mephisto" (July 1945), but even these revealed a tired, written-out Gibson, by now recycling ideas and situations from earlier novels. Following a salary dispute, he left the series quite abruptly after completing "Malmordo" (July 1946), a slightly-above-average thriller.

The final issue of The Shadow's pulp magazine — number 325, to be exact!

Fellow magician/writer Bruce Elliott, who had written some Shadow backup stories featuring retooled dime-novel hero Nick Carter, was drafted to replace Gibson. His 15 additions to the canon are held in low esteem by pulp devotees, and not entirely without reason. In most of them, The Shadow barely appeared; Lamont Cranston carried the action, such as it was, all by himself. Streamlined to 30,000 words, the Elliott Shadows were found in the back of the magazine. Newly appointed editor Babette Rosmond, no fan of hero pulps, did everything she could to diminish The Shadow in his own publication. Now a bi-monthly titled *Shadow Mystery*, its main character no longer featured on covers, the once trend-setting magazine continued to decline. In 1948 Rosmond quit and both *Shadow* and *Doc Savage* were then entrusted to Daisy Bacon, long-time editor of *Love Story Magazine*, which had once been Street & Smith's top-selling pulp.

On Bacon's watch the magazine's title was changed to *The Shadow*. She rehired Gibson and gave him a free hand. Bacon also persuaded Ralston to restore the magazines to their pre-war dimensions in an attempt to recapture the spirit of their glory days. The revival failed, however, and with the Summer 1949 issue, featuring "The Whispering Eyes," The Shadow retired. From pulp magazines, that is. As a radio character, he continued to fight crime for another five years.

I don't particularly like any post-war Shadow novels, but the best of a bad lot have to be Elliott's last, "Reign of Terror" (July 1948), and Gibson's first upon returning, "Jade Dragon" (September 1948). Written under Bacon's direction, they reversed the drastic changes Rosmond had insisted upon. Neither can be considered a classic Shadow adventure, but if you feel obliged to read one from this disappointing period, either will suffice.

The influence of *The Shadow Magazine* cannot be overstated. Most pulps featured the adventures of series heroes; the presence of such reader favorites had long been accepted as a valuable circulation-building tool. But conventional wisdom held that readers craved variety and would no longer regularly buy a sheet devoted almost entirely to the exploits of a single character. The gradual decline and eventual termination of the nickel weeklies had proven that—or so it was thought.

The first issue of Street & Smith's *The Shadow, A Detective Magazine* had been on the nation's newsstands for only a couple months when the May 11, 1931 *Film Daily* carried an announcement listing the upcoming season's slate of releases by the Universal Pictures Corporation. (A movie-industry "season" at that time ran from approximately Labor Day through early June.) Among the 104 short subjects named for issuance during the 1931-32 year

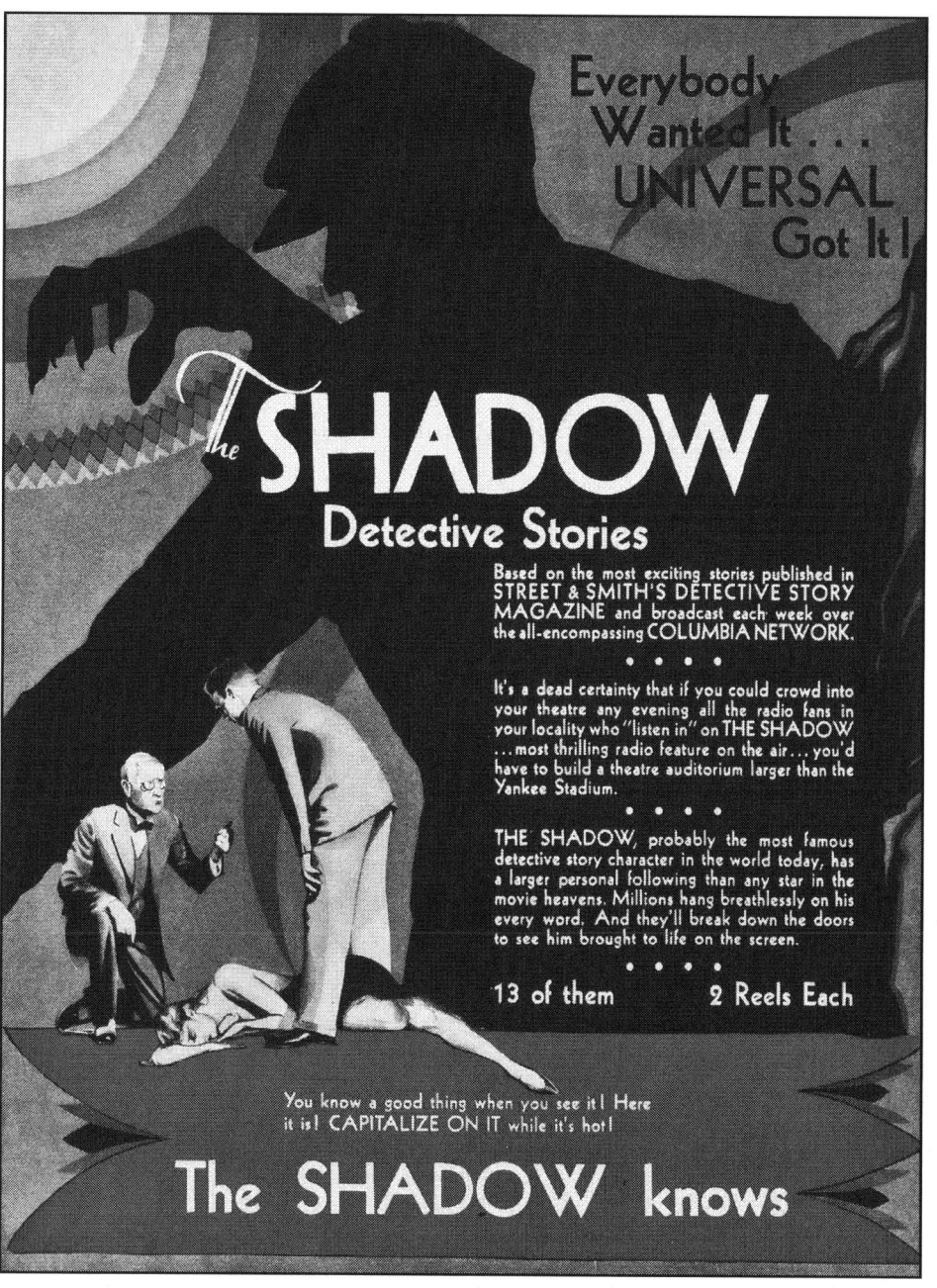

This full-page advertisement appeared in Universal's "campaign book" produced for exhibitors to help them decide which of the studio's offerings they wanted to rent for the upcoming motion-picture "season" (in this case, 1931-32). Despite the hyperbole in the ad copy, it's evident that Universal believed theater men would be aware of the radio program and stumble over each other trying to book the Shadow Detective featurettes. Note that the studio planned to release 13 of them.

This frame capture from *Burglar to the Rescue* has The Shadow's first moment on a movie screen. That's radio's Shadow, Frank Readick, wearing the hat, mask and cloak he also donned for many publicity photos during his long association with the character.

were 13 "Shadow Detective" featurettes. Obviously, these "two-reelers" had no connection to the pulp magazine; they were to be adaptations of episodes from radio's *Detective Story Hour*, which every Thursday night dramatized short stories from Street & Smith's *Detective Story Magazine*.

As is well known today, The Shadow was created (by writer Harry Charlot) to host these crime dramas, his periodic interjections designed as scene transitions and his declarations that "crime does not pay" calculated to frighten potential malefactors. Several actors played the character in the show's early months, but Frank Readick's sepulchral tones resonated best with listeners. The *Detective Story Hour* quickly became a national sensation—not so much for the individual stories, which were entertaining but unremarkable, but for The Shadow himself, whose creepy laughter sent chills up the spines of people huddled around their radios. Silent movies, of course, would not have been the proper medium for screen adaptations of such adventures, but the relatively new talking pictures were ideal for such a purpose, and the two-reeler (with its running time of 18 to 22 minutes) seemed appropriate, length-wise, for translating *Detective Story Hour* adaptations to celluloid.

The first featurette was obviously shot in Universal's New York studio; the cast members were all Broadway actors and several were appearing in stage productions during the period it had to have been made. *A Burglar to the Rescue*, based on the *Detective Story Magazine* short of the same title by Herman Landon, unfolded on one set—the office of a small-town banker—whose cramped dimensions and perfunctory lighting are certainly representative of other shorts lensed in the Big Apple at that time.

Written and directed by George Cochrane, the brother of Universal president Carl Laemmle's right-hand man, *Burglar* was released nationally

To promote the films they were showing in their theaters, exhibitors received "lobby cards" that could be spotted in frames on their lobby walls. This "title card" mistakenly refers to the first Shadow featurette as "*The* Burglar" rather than "*A* Burglar."

on September 7, 1931. Long believed lost, it was found and preserved by Universal's vault manager some years ago. This first Shadow featurette introduces viewers to Steven Corley (Thurston Hall), the president of a small-town bank, who has been appropriating the funds to support his extravagant but honest girlfriend Marian (Charlotte Wynters). One night as he's cooking the books, after entertaining the gal pal, Corley is visited by a gun-wielding intruder named Holtz (Frank Shannon, who later played Dr. Zarkov in Universal's Flash Gordon serials), a man with a leveled gun. The banker welcomes the arrival of this apparent thief, who can obliterate any signs of Corley's embezzling by cleaning out the vault. The stranger identifies himself as an escaped convict, and later it develops that he was actually Jack Dunning, a cashier whom the president framed into prison for his own pilfering. Ironically, hick constable Andy Hurley (Arthur Aylesworth) shows up just in time to accuse Corley of Dunning's theft and take him away—proving that, as The Shadow intones, crime does not pay.

By today's standards, *A Burglar to the Rescue* is incredibly crude. Truth be told, it was crude by 1931 standards too. The early New York-made talkies were undeniably inferior technically to those shot in Hollywood. But with Tinseltown plants kept occupied with the making of more profitable feature films, short-subject production remained concentrated in New York for much of the decade. Fox, Paramount, Universal, Warner Brothers, and the newly minted RKO Radio all maintained sound stages on the east coast.

Burglar's significance to Shadow fans is twofold. To begin with, the character is visualized for the first time, superimposed over a *Detective Story Magazine* cover. He wears a black fedora and long cloak, with a domino mask partially covering his features, and appears as a shadow projected on a wall or, in one shot, is photographed head-on in silhouette. Remember, in

Thurston Hall and Charlotte Wynters— who were frequently seen in Thirties films— are shown in this scene from *Burglar to the Rescue*. Wynters later married popular character actor Barton MacLane.

September 1931 the Master of Darkness as described in Walter B. Gibson's novels had not yet been pictured on a pulp magazine's cover. Interior illustrations were vague, although some showed him wearing a cape. And early publicity photos taken to promote the radio show had depicted actor James La Curto in a cowled cloak with no hat. So *Burglar to the Rescue* scores points on the basis of iconographic evolution.

More importantly, The Shadow's voice in this film is obviously that of Frank Readick. Since his *Detective Story Hour* episodes are all lost to the ages, this humble two-reeler gives present-day fans their only opportunity to hear him in character, to appreciate the sinister cackling that defined The Shadow for millions of listeners. (It also was the laugh referenced by Gibson in the pulp novels.) Otherwise, *Burglar* does not impress today's spectator; it hinges on the irony of the ex-convict getting Corley arrested for the same crime he earlier framed onto the innocent cashier. The acting will impress most as stiff and unconvincing, although some of this awkwardness can be attributed to stage performers coping with primitive sound-recording techniques. Those film buffs predisposed to enjoy creaky early talkies are likely to be more forgiving and might enjoy it more.

Reaction to the first Shadow featurette was mixed. *Film Daily*'s review was complimentary. "Initial subject in the Shadow Detective series is built up with a lot of creepy suspense by the employment of a shadow projected every so often throughout the action, with the voice of the shadow forecasting the retribution that awaits the criminal," wrote the anonymous critic. "The climax is dramatic and carries a good kick. . . . [T]he mystery and suspense is strong throughout, and well handled for thrills."

For reasons unknown, the remaining shorts in the series were shot in Hollywood on the Universal lot. Mainstream film actors and directors

Banker Corley winds up in prison and is taunted by The Shadow at the end of *Burglar to the Rescue*.

participate in the later entries, although Frank Readick was left behind in New York. In my opinion, losing him was a major blow to the series. Since The Shadow's portrayer got no screen credit and the Hollywood-made entries were not available until just recently, it's been impossible to ascertain his identity. Personally, I believe him to be one of two character actors who were incredibly prolific in the early talkie period: either Frank Sheridan or DeWitt Jennings. These middle-aged men typically played blustery characters, and since the Hollywood Shadow is louder and harsher than Readick, I'm inclined to vote for one of them based on my familiarity with their voices (which are remarkably similar).

Although the shorts had been budgeted at $10,000 each and allotted three days for principal photography—standard for such productions—the second Shadow Detective featurette, *Trapped*, went over schedule and over budget. Martin Grams, who delved into Universal records while researching his excellent 2011 book, *The Shadow, The History and Mystery of the Radio Program, 1930-1954*, learned that *Trapped* took four days to shoot and had a negative cost of $12,696. The overage was not insignificant, because short subjects at that time were typically rented to exhibitors for two to five dollars each. Overshooting the budget by, say, three thousand dollars might force a studio to secure a thousand additional bookings just to maintain the same profit margin.

Trapped, which also exists, was an improvement in terms of lighting, photography, sound recording, and general production value. By this time the series had been entrusted to Stanley Bergerman (another Laemmle relative), who delegated day-to-day production responsibilities to Bryan Foy, scion of the famous theatrical family. German-born Kurt Neumann, who would become one of Hollywood's most prolific directors of "B" pictures in

For *Trapped*, the second Shadow Detective short, production was moved to Universal's West Coast facility in Universal City. Top-billed Lina Basquette later claimed to have kicked Adolf Hitler in the groin when he made a pass at her during her short-lived 1937 engagement at a studio in Germany.

all genres, was hired to helm the rest of the series and handled the megaphone on all but one of the remaining entries.

Trapped finds a female investigator named Joan (played by Lina Basquette) going undercover to get evidence proving that gangster Tony Valisimo (Stanley Fields) committed a murder for which young Jimmy Dare (James Murray) has been framed. Joan is even prepared to marry Valisimo, and events are about to spiral out of control when the arrest is finally made and Detective Jack Reed (Jason Robards Sr.) liberated from a tough spot.

The second Shadow Detective featurette was not well received by critics working for the important movie-industry trade papers. These publications were carefully read by exhibitors, who often gave disproportionate weight to the reviews. One can only guess how many prospective customers shied away from *Trapped* after reading the notices.

Film Daily's anonymous scribe said, "This starts out as a mystery, trying to unravel a murder, but pretty soon it proves to be just another gangster picture, and a very poor one at that. It is filled with inconsistencies and loose threads that never tie up intelligently."

The *Motion Picture Herald* reviewer agreed. "[S]uspense and real dramatic action are rather woefully lacking. A shadow of a man appears on the screen at odd moments and at the opening and conclusion of the piece, pointing out in a deep voice that the ways of evil lead to jail, the gallows, or something equally unpleasant."

Sealed Lips, the third short, went before cameras during the first week in October and was released the following month. Based on a Donald Van Riper yarn in *Detective Story Magazine*, it revolved around Buzz Stanwyck (silent-serial star Walter Miller), who seemed to have engineered the elusive "perfect alibi." It was no better received than *Trapped*, and critics were

From left to right: *Trapped* principal players James Murray, Stanley Fields, and Lina Basquette. To save money the Shadow featurettes were deliberately written to feature small casts and a limited number of settings.

beginning to carp about The Shadow's presence. (Clearly, these were not folks who were familiar with the radio program.) *Film Daily* summarized the featurette thusly: "All about a theatrical owner who plans the murder of his manager, who is his rival in love. He builds up an alibi through employing a makeup artist to act as his double. There is plenty of action, but the mystery element is lacking. They use the device of the 'shadow,' who appears every so often and points [to] the moral that crime does not pay. This seems to serve no good purpose, and is an amateurish touch."

Motion Picture Herald reported that "Three murders in the first reel start things moving, but story loses out because of shadow figure who imposes itself at regular intervals to declare in throaty tones a warning against crime."

House of Mystery, released to theaters shortly before Christmas of 1931, is the strongest of the four Shadow shorts that have been preserved. Adapted from a pulp story by Park Avenue Hunt Club creator Judson Philips, it has good stormy-night-in-the-old-dark-house atmosphere and one genuinely shocking sequence in which a woman (Geneva Mitchell) plunges to her death through a trap door. Two hunters, a sheriff (Wilfred Lucas) and his close friend (Leland Hodgson) practically stumble onto the crime scene and solve the mystery, despite efforts at obfuscation by the chief suspect's wealthy father (James Durkin).

Film Daily continued its vendetta against the Shadow Detective series in its appraisal of *House of Mystery*. "The plot has plenty of tenseness and mystery, and moves swiftly to a rather novel climax," the reviewer grudgingly admitted. "But we still think that this series would be improved by eliminating the 'Shadow' with his demoniac laugh, who comes into the picture ever so often to point the finger of fate at the criminal. His laugh is

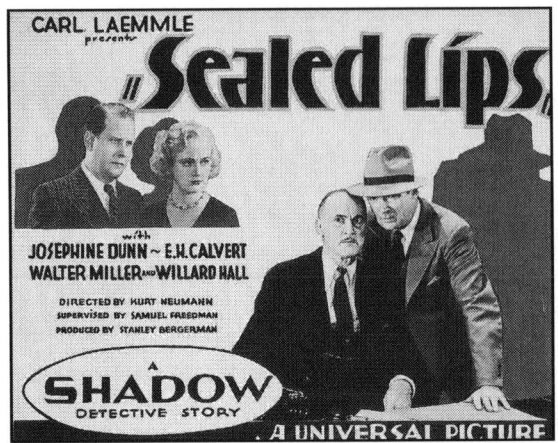

Sealed Lips cast members E. H. Calvert and Walter Miller had previously worked together in a 1928 serial, *The Man Without a Face*, in which Calvert was revealed as the villain by hero Miller in the final episode.

ghastly and poor stuff for the kids to listen to, as well as for any high-strung woman." Fans of The Shadow on radio would respectfully disagree.

The Red Shadow, released on January 20, 1932, brought back Walter Miller, this time as a detective investigating the murder of a recently married millionaire who was about to dismiss his servants at the behest of his new wife. A stolen necklace figures in the action as well. Typically, the critics weren't impressed. *Film Daily* opined, "It doesn't take too long to guess the guilty person in this detective drama. The story, taken from a popular detective magazine, suffers from lack of suspense."

The sixth and final short in the Shadow Detective series was *The Circus Show-Up*, released on February 17, 1932. Experienced director Lewis Seiler—who had helmed one of Tom Mix's very best Westerns for Fox, *The Great K&A Train Robbery* (1926)—did his best with a poorly developed adaptation of Leslie T. White's original pulp yarn. It had novelty value for casting two of Loretta Young's sisters: Polly Ann Young as Irene Duval, trapeze artist and murder victim, and Sally Blane as one of the suspects. Production values were almost non-existent, with most sequences consisting of people standing in front of canvas backdrops and talking. It limped into release on February 17.

Up to this point Universal had stuck to its announced schedule, releasing a new Shadow featurette every four weeks. But mid-March came and went with no seventh installment, and the March 27 issue of *Film Daily*, carrying a report on recent activity at Universal City, noted that the series had been curtailed after six entries.

Why did the Shadow Detective featurettes fail when the radio show was so popular? That's hard to say. The series' overall quality—or lack of same—probably had something to do with it. Radio listeners, after all, could

E. H. Calvert questions Josephine Dunn and Willard Hall in this tense scene from the third Shadow Detective series entry, which was not very well received.

imagine more lavish sets and backgrounds than the films could show on their paltry budgets. Hard-core film buffs can take pleasure in the casts, which all include wonderful "B"-movie character actors, but no first-rate talents appeared in the series. And while Kurt Neumann, who helmed four of the six shorts, eventually became a solid if uninventive director, these early efforts—with the possible exception of *House of Mystery*—clearly represent the work of an apprentice.

Then, too, the loss of Frank Readick hurt the films. The Shadow as voiced in the Hollywood-shot entries simply was not as impressive. Moreover, while the character had been used well in *Burglar to the Rescue*, subsequent installments employed him less effectively, sometimes tossing him a single line to be followed by a chuckle. Clearly, though, the moviegoing public had rejected The Shadow as a screen presence. It was another five years before he again graced America's movie theaters.

Why Hollywood took so long to revisit the character is a greater mystery than any The Shadow faced in his pulp adventures. Although the *Detective Story Hour* underwent title and format changes over a period of several years, The Shadow's presence remained constant and his blood-curdling voice was heard by millions of listeners.

By 1936 the Master of Darkness was off the air—temporarily—but his magazine maintained its hold on the reading public. That same year saw the incorporation of a new production-distribution entity in Hollywood: Grand National Films. The brainchild of former film-exchange manager Edward L. Alperson, Grand National came into existence as a consequence of the ongoing Depression, which forced exhibitors to offer double-feature programs as an inducement to cash-strapped patrons. Mid-Thirties moviegoers demanded more for the few dimes they could afford to spend

Walter Miller was back for the fifth Shadow short, this time playing a detective investigating the murder of a millionaire who was planning to dismiss his servants at the behest of his new wife.

on entertainment, and the competition for their business was keen. They were willing to endure a few stinkers now and then, but not many.

The major studios owned theater chains and produced grade "B" films to fill the double-feature programs exhibited in their downtown picture palaces. But most of the nation's movie screens were found in small towns, semi-rural areas, and the "neighborhood houses" of bedroom communities in big cities. So there was great demand for "B" pictures. Independent producers along Hollywood's Poverty Row met that demand in the Depression's early years, but those perpetually under-capitalized entrepreneurs lacked the one thing Edward Alperson had assembled: a distribution network consisting of 30 exchanges in key markets across the country.

For marquee allure Grand National had James Cagney, who left Warner Brothers in late 1935 following a contract dispute. The bantam star wanted creative control and profit participation; by granting him both, Alperson secured the services of a top box-office draw that normally would have been beyond the reach of a new studio with limited resources.

In 1937, series films—especially fast-moving "B" pictures with detective characters—were extremely popular. Paramount had Bulldog Drummond; Warners had Perry Mason and Torchy Blane; Fox had Charlie Chan and Mr. Moto. Alperson thought he could cash in on this trend and acquired screen rights to several well-known fictional characters.

Grand National's promotional copy in that year's *Film Daily Product Guide and Directors Annual* promised 65 feature films for the 1937-38 season. Among them were 16 entries in four separate series featuring Maxwell Grant's The Shadow, George Harmon Coxe's Flash Casey, Laurie York Erskine's Renfrew of the Royal Mounted, and Albert Richard Wetjen's Wallaby Jim of the Islands. The four Shadow movies, listed in order of

Walter Miller doesn't seem to trust Harriet Lorraine, and we're not sure we blame him — she looks like a woman with lots to hide. Could she be the killer of her husband?

planned release, were to be *The Shadow Strikes, The Shadow's Disguise, The Shadow in Panama,* and *The Shadow in Society*.

Alperson assigned the licensed characters to various producers supplying movies to Grand National. Sibling filmmakers Max and Arthur Alexander, nephews of Universal president Carl Laemmle, assumed responsibility for the Shadow and Flash Casey series. Still in their twenties, the Alexanders specialized in cheap Westerns and had just completed a sextet of quickie horse operas with cowboy star Rex Bell, better known in Hollywood as the husband of erstwhile "It Girl" Clara Bow. The brothers' company, Colony Pictures, was headquartered on Sunset Boulevard in Hollywood. Another Laemmle relative, Alfred Stern, served as general manager and production supervisor. Colony was a lean operation, even given its Poverty Row status and the Alexanders' meager resources.

The brothers hired third-rate screenwriters Al Martin and Rex Taylor to adapt Walter Gibson's "The Ghost of the Manor," published in the June 15, 1933 issue of *The Shadow Magazine* and one of four stories obtained from Street & Smith in the licensing agreement. Martin's shooting script was polished by veteran scenarist John Krafft, who did not receive screen credit for his contribution.

Not willing to rely solely on The Shadow's popularity for the success of their maiden effort as Grand National producers, the Alexanders searched for a star who had box-office appeal but could be hired for peanuts. They selected silent-era leading man Rod La Rocque, a Cecil B. De Mille protégé whose career had fizzled out shortly after the advent of talking pictures. La Rocque was eager to make a comeback, even if it meant starring in "B" pictures. He agreed to do the four Shadow films for a reported $10,000, or $2,500 each—a fraction of the salary he had commanded in his prime.

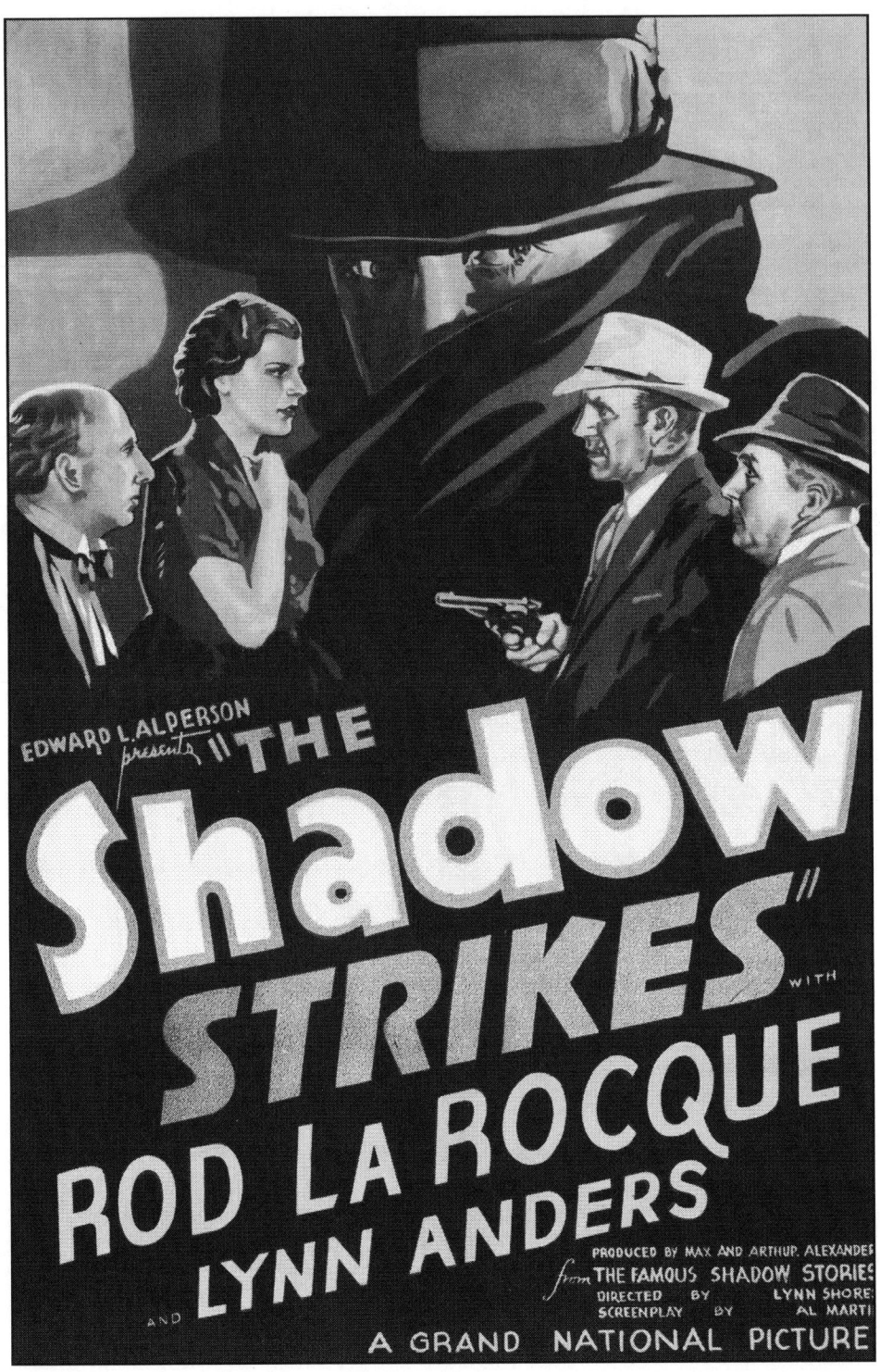

This "one-sheet" poster lured moviegoers into theaters playing this Shadow film.

Silent-era star Rod La Rocque was rather improbably cast as the 1937 Shadow.

For the ingénue role Max and Arthur chose Agnes Anderson, a pretty brunette with a half-dozen bit parts to her credit. They saw potential in the 23-year-old actress, changed her name to Lynn Anders, and promised her a big publicity buildup. The supporting cast was filled out with Poverty Row regulars, including silent-screen favorites Walter McGrail, Kenneth Harlan, John Elliott, Norman Ainsley, and John St. Polis.

The picture's direction was entrusted to Lynn Shores, a competent but uninspired journeyman possibly hired because he knew the star, having helmed *The Delightful Rogue*, a 1929 La Rocque vehicle.

Principal photography began on April 26, 1937. Shooting was completed on May 9. During this period the film had several working titles, including *The Shadow, Mr. Shadow,* and *Alias The Shadow.* Colony's financial records are long gone, so it is impossible to know exactly how much was spent on the first Shadow feature. Judging by the evident production values and based on my knowledge of Poverty Row filmmaking, I'd say it was brought in for $40,000 or less. At that time, the least expensive "B" pictures from major studios (barring Westerns) cost a minimum of $75,000. By any standards *The Shadow Strikes* was a cheapie.

The film introduces Lamont Cranston as an amateur criminologist whose war against crime is motivated by his desire to identify the murderer of his father, a prominent lawyer and "one of the finest men who ever lived."

Winstead Comstock (center, Walter McGrail) has just been murdered. From left to right: Humphrey Comstock (Bill Kellogg), Marcia Delthern (Lynn Anders), Lamont Cranston (Rod La Rocque), Jasper Delthern (James Blakeley), Captain Breen (Kenneth Harlan), and Warren Berranger (John Carnivale). Whodunit?

While prowling one night as The Shadow, garbed in black hat and cloak, he interrupts the burglary of an office belonging to attorney Chester Randall. The timely arrival of Police Captain Breen (Kenneth Harlan) forces Cranston to hide his Shadow disguise and pretend to be Randall. While posing as the lawyer he accepts a call from elderly millionaire Caleb Delthern (John St. Polis), who wants his will changed immediately.

With Breen at his elbow, Cranston reluctantly agrees and hurries off to the Delthern estate, where he is instructed by the old man—who is not personally acquainted with Randall—to compose a new will disinheriting his niece Marcia (Lynn Anders). She is engaged to Warren Barringer (John Carnivale), of whom Caleb does not approve. When the millionaire is subsequently murdered in his study, suspicion falls on the newly designated heir, Marcia's cousin Winstead Comstock (Walter McGrail). Not long thereafter, Winstead himself is shot dead, and the police train their wary eyes on Marcia's brother, Jasper (James Blakeley), a young wastrel heavily indebted to Brossett (Cy Kendall), gambling-house proprietor and secret head of a criminal gang. Cranston, still posing as lawyer Randall, eventually ferrets out the real murderer. The picture ends as it began, with the crime fighter seated at his desk, staring at the bullet he hopes will some day lead to his father's killer.

Cranston (center) tries to reassure Marcia and her brother that things will work out.

"The Ghost of the Manor" was one of Walter Gibson's periodic attempts to trade on the popularity of John Willard's 1922 Broadway smash, *The Cat and the Canary*, which took place in an old dark house and revolved around suspicious heirs to a dead man's fortune. *Shadow Strikes* adapters Martin, Taylor and Krafft retained Gibson's theme, setting, and some of the characters but made significant alterations to his plot. The murderer's identity and motive were changed, and Warren Barringer, Gibson's Proxy Hero, became one of the primary suspects.

The modifications to "Ghost of the Manor" wouldn't have mattered if *The Shadow Strikes* had turned out well. Unfortunately, it suffered from muddled scripting, flaccid direction, and somnolent performances. La Rocque, in his younger days an engaging performer, seemed bored with the role and embarrassed by his scenes in Shadow garb. His line readings were flat and he failed to imbue the character with the necessary aura of mystery. Lynn Anders seemed to be trying harder but she was wooden and, despite her general attractiveness, lacking in sex appeal. She acted on stage under her real name, Agnes Anderson, and later married writer Budd Schulberg.

The direction by Lynn Shores was perfunctory at best. He made few attempts to achieve effects that might have lent an eerie atmosphere to the proceedings. Continuity errors were rampant, one of the worst being Cranston's identification as "Granston" in a newspaper article shown on screen following the killer's climactic unveiling.

Breen and Cranston interrogate the suspicious butler, Wellington (Wilson Benge).

Most disturbing was the film's lack of fidelity to accepted Shadow lore. For example, *The Shadow Strikes* never even hinted at what the magazine's readers knew for certain: that The Shadow impersonated Lamont Cranston, not the other way around. Moreover, the pulp's popular recurring characters—Police Commissioner Ralph Weston, Inspector Joe Cardona, and The Shadow's many agents—were conspicuous by their absence. Cranston's butler, identified in the novels as Richards, was inexplicably renamed Hendricks for his screen turn.

Grand National screened *The Shadow Strikes* for trade-paper critics in early July, shortly before the film was originally scheduled for release. It was not well received. The *Motion Picture Herald*'s scribe tried to be kind but betrayed a noticeable lack of enthusiasm: "A trail at least has been opened for the exhibitor by the development of the character, The Shadow, in printer's ink and radio voice. . . . The sparse comment in any direction after the New York pre-showing in a projection room indicated acceptability without enthusiasm." Other normally forgiving reviewers savaged the picture. Leading the charge was *Variety*'s "Wear," usually inclined to be charitable toward low-budget indies. "*The Shadow Strikes* is unmistakably flotsam," he declared in his July 14th notice. "[W]hat might have been an

The Shadow makes an unusual daytime excursion in this scene from *The Shadow Strikes*. The Al Martin script was written in such a way as to minimize Lamont Cranston's appearances in character, although the cloaked figure was prominently featured in the film's advertising and promotional materials. According to one source, star Rod La Rocque felt that The Shadow was too "hokey" for an actor of his stature. This might explain why he totally eschewed the black hat and cloak in the sequel, *International Crime*. But it's likely that audiences who knew the character from his pulp magazine resented not seeing the hero in his customary garb.

entertaining sleuth yarn is marred by stupid dialog, feeble acting, misdirection, and dangling continuity. When the film goes mysterious, the point is smothered beyond recognition, and when it is not following the detective slant, the yarn becomes extremely boring."

After going on to complain about the directing and cinematography, Wear took aim at the star: "Rod La Rocque has not been afforded a happy vehicle for his return to screen prominence. He looks much older but strains valiantly to put life into this phony 'Shadow' character."

Perhaps disappointed by such harsh notices, Grand National postponed the film's release until October, with the 1937-38 season already well underway. Alperson's struggling firm gave *The Shadow Strikes* as big a publicity boost as Grand National's limited resources allowed. Street & Smith plugged the movie in *The Shadow Magazine* and, for the only time in the title's history, using a photo cover in place of the usual painted cover. It adorned the November 1, 1937 issue, which hit newsstands a couple weeks

prior to the film's national release. Oddly, it wasn't La Rocque in the photo but Street & Smith's assistant art director Bill Lawlor, who resembled Cranston as described by Walter Gibson.

The "Blue Coal" people (D.L. & W. Coal Company), sponsors of the Shadow radio program, did their best to promote the film by offering a free ton of coal to exhibitors who played *The Shadow Strikes*.

Exhibitors were disappointed in the film and didn't hesitate to say so. They opined in such trade-paper columns as the *Motion Picture Herald*'s "What the Picture Did for Me" that Grand National had bungled what should have been a sure-fire box-office winner. Harry M. Palmer, manager of the Temple Court Theatre in Washington, Indiana, wrote: "Not strong enough to stand alone, but will fit in on any double-feature program. It is pleasing entertainment. Some of our customers are asking for the second in this 'Shadow' series." He was an exception, though.

The initial series entry was not yet playing its first-run engagements when Max and Arthur Alexander began preparing the next installment, previously announced as *The Shadow's Disguise* but retitled *Return of The Shadow* in late July. John Krafft, uncredited contributor to the *Shadow Strikes* screenplay, was assigned to adapt "Foxhound," the second Shadow novel

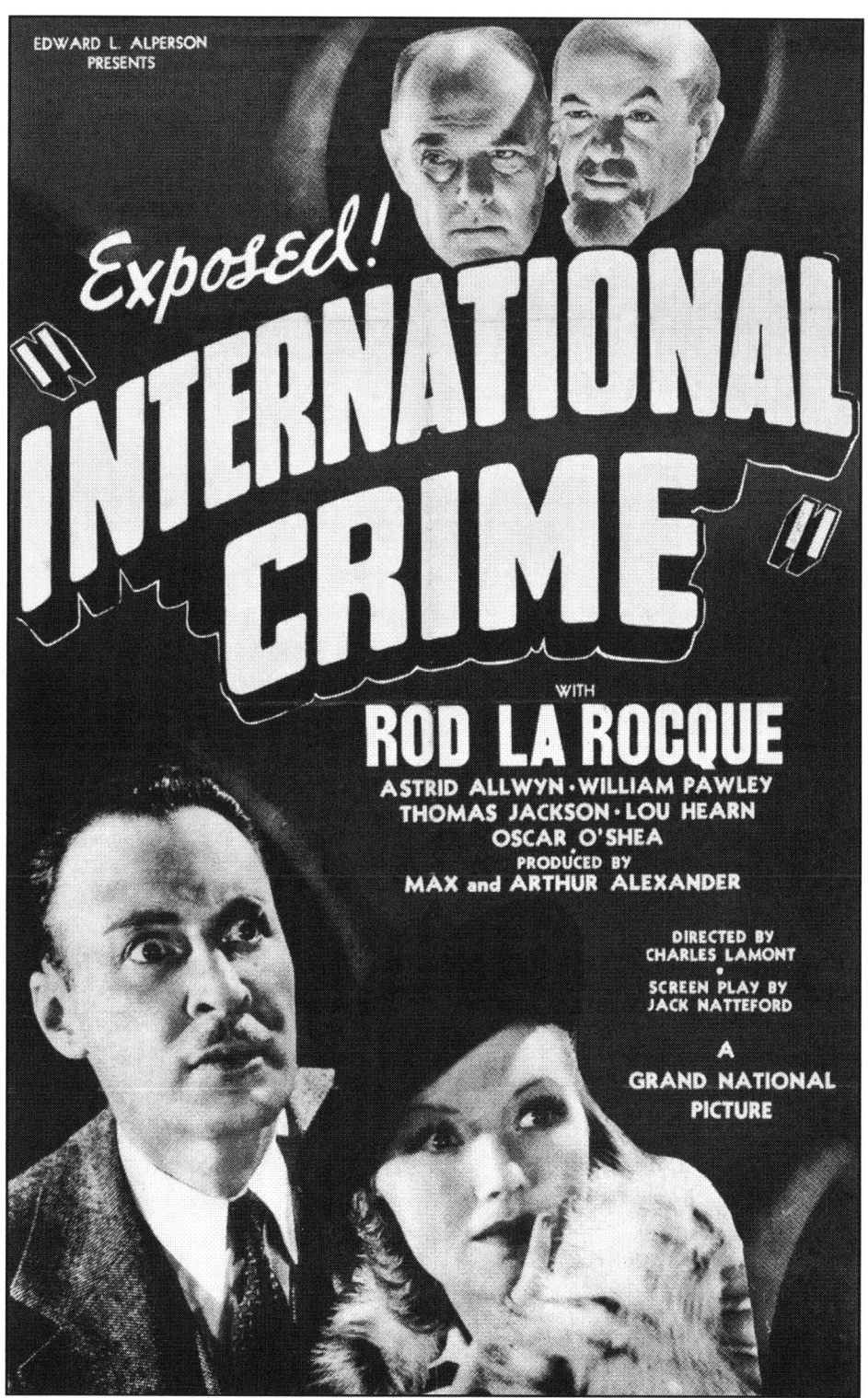

International Crime (1938), unlike its predecessor, reflected the influence of the already-wildly-popular Shadow radio program, as indicated by the presence of Shrevvy (Lew Hearn, left) and Margot Lane (Astrid Allwyn), inexplicably renamed "Phoebe." Cranston was introduced as a radio crime reporter nicknamed "The Shadow."

written by Theodore Tinsley under the Maxwell Grant byline typically reserved for Walter Gibson. Published in *The Shadow Magazine*'s January 15, 1937 issue, this fast-moving yarn began with the trial of a killer acquitted thanks to his crooked lawyer. Later it introduced a mysterious master criminal and concentrated on the aftermath of a twenty-million-dollar heist.

Krafft took the easy way out: He jettisoned Tinsley's plot and substituted one of his own devising. Long-time screenwriter Jack Natteford prepared a shooting script based on Krafft's original story. (Strangely, the finished film bore no writing credits at all.) Charles Lamont, a prolific helmer of Poverty Row features, had recently been hired by Alperson and was assigned to give the second Shadow movie some much-needed pizzazz. He was accustomed to working fast and on tight budgets, so the Alexanders were happy to have him.

The brothers couldn't seem to stick with a title for the second entry. A notice in the November 6 issue of *Motion Picture Herald* indicated that the film was just about to go before the cameras and referred to it as *Return of The Shadow*. The December 6, 1937 issue of *Hollywood Reporter* carried a notice that principal photography on what was now called *The Shadow Speaks* had just gotten underway. Like its predecessor, Colony's second Shadow film was shot in two weeks. Subsequent press reports referred to it as *The Shadow Murder Case*. Post-production work, delayed until after the holiday season, was completed early in 1938. By early April the second Shadow opus was called *International Crime*. Why, you might ask, substitute a title that didn't include The Shadow's name? Here's my theory: By the time the second series entry had been edited and scored, disappointing box-office returns from the first were trickling in. I believe Grand National got cold feet and decided to market the film as a standalone mystery, not part of a

While broadcasting from his private studio, Cranston entertains an unwelcome visitor: a notorious crook known as "Honest John" (William Pawley), who wants The Shadow to prove him innocent of robbery and murder of an international financier involved with spies.

highly touted series. The sequel's posters make no mention of The Shadow, which backs up my contention.

International Crime depicts Lamont Cranston as a Walter Winchell-like columnist and broadcaster working for the *Evening Classic* as "The Shadow." One of his regular listeners is Police Commissioner Weston (Thomas Jackson), who considers Cranston a nuisance. While investigating an explosion at the home of international financier Gerald Morton, killed during an apparent attempt to rob his safe, The Shadow infuriates Weston, who has him jailed as a material witness in retaliation. Cranston's ditzy assistant, Phoebe Lane (Astrid Allwyn), and his personal cab driver Moe (Lew Hearn) bail the columnist out in time for his next broadcast, during which the principal suspect, a notorious safecracker nicknamed "Honest John" (William Pawley), bursts into the studio and forces The Shadow at gunpoint to clear his name.

Later, Morton's brother and partner, Roger (John St. Polis), threatens Cranston with legal action for implying that the murdered man was involved in crooked dealings. Cranston and Phoebe become acquainted with Germanic foreigners named Flotow (William von Brincken) and Starkhov (Tenen Holtz). Eventually they uncover evidence suggesting a connection between these men and the late Gerald Morton. Joined by Honest John, who's trying to reform, The Shadow has Moe drive them to Roger Morton's house, where Flotow and Storkhov are about to steal $100,000 in negotiable bonds. They plan to finance a revolution and confess to framing the murder of Gerald after he discovered their intentions. The Shadow and Honest John apprehend the conspirators as they are trying to force Roger to commit suicide. Weston and his men arrive to arrest the villains into custody, leaving Cranston to break the story on his evening broadcast.

Cranston, posing as an international crook, runs afoul of Starkhov (Tenen Holtz), one of the conspirators responsible for the murder of financier Gerald Morton.

Variety reviewer "Char" had surprisingly kind words for *International Crime*. "A crime thriller of fair program value for double bills on which it will prove passable as the number two feature," he called it, adding: "The Alexander brothers have given their 'meller' good backgrounds, considerable movement of action, suspense, and some romantic flavor, plus a few splotches of comedy. While occasionally too much is given over to detail and occasionally some liberties are taken, on the whole the interest is well held."

Film Daily opined that the film "makes enjoyable entertainment," adding: "As a single [feature] it can play secondary houses, and it should do very nicely as support in better grade duals [double-feature houses]. . . . In the independent field it is one of the better shows."

Gus McCarthy's review for *Motion Picture Herald* characterized the film as "majoring in melodramatic theatricals, although not without a respectable quota of comedy and romance [and] held together by suspense and semi-mystery."

International Crime had several ties to the Shadow of pulp and radio fame. Commissioner Weston finally reached the big screen, and one of Cranston's assistants, named Burke, might well have been Clyde Burke, one of the pulp Shadow's most trusted agents. Cranston's personal cab driver was identified in dialogue only as "Moe," but publicity materials referred to him as Moe Shrevnitz. Scatterbrained Phoebe Lane probably owed her inclusion in the film to Grand National's acknowledgment of the new Shadow radio program, which debuted on September 26, 1937 with the Master of Darkness as its protagonist and gave him one Margot Lane as a trusted friend and companion. (The substitution of "Phoebe" for "Margot" makes no sense and has never been explained.) Screenwriters Natteford and Krafft seemed at least nominally familiar with the radio series.

The title card for Grand National's second Shadow opus is well designed, but notice that nowhere will one see any mention of The Shadow, and the black-garbed figure familiar to readers of the pulp magazine is conspicuous by his absence — deliberately.

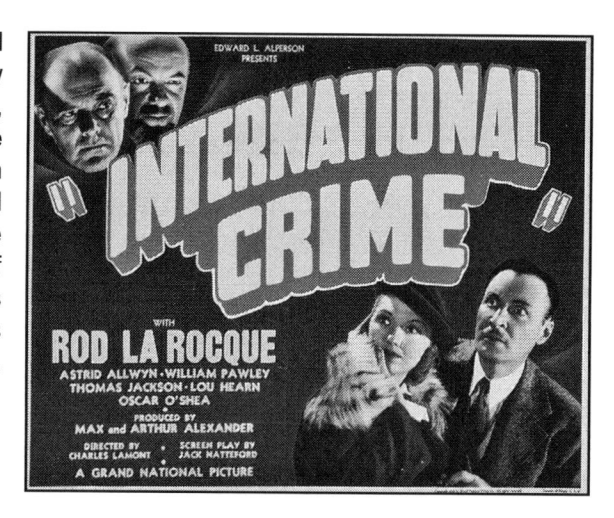

International Crime did, however, deviate from the Shadow canon in major ways. Most egregiously, its Lamont Cranston never donned the familiar hat or cloak, "The Shadow" being nothing more than a byline. Nonetheless, the movie established him as something of a cult figure. A number of young boys, listening intently to one of his broadcasts, were seen wearing badges emblazoned with the pen-and-ink profile used as an identifying symbol of the magazine's Shadow Club. (A larger, poorly rendered version of that portrait hung on the wall of Cranston's office.) Eagle-eyed viewers might have spotted a copy of *The Shadow Magazine*'s April 1, 1934 issue on a desk in front of one gum-chewing lad.

International Crime was a better film than its predecessor, albeit not by much. The pace was brisk, the dialogue snappier, and the performances livelier. La Rocque still did not seem well cast as an ace crime fighter, but he was more energetic as the newspaper columnist than as the torpid Cranston of *The Shadow Strikes*.

Unfortunately—or fortunately, depending on one's opinion of these Grand National efforts—*International Crime* fared no better at the nation's box offices than the previous Shadow movie. By late 1938 declining film rentals and diminishing exhibitor interest persuaded Grand National president Alperson to suspend all series production. Colony's Flash Casey series never got past the opener; *Here's Flash Casey* (1937), another botch job, disrespected the source material. The Wallaby Jim series did likewise. Producer/director Al Herman completed two Renfrew of the Royal Mounted movies before Alperson pulled the plug, although he subsequently struck a distribution deal with Monogram Pictures and continued the series for that small company.

Grand National's Shadow series tanked for one reason: The first two entries simply were not good enough. Patrons of small-town theaters and neighborhood houses still craved "B" pictures with recurring characters, but the Shadow, Renfrew, and Flash Casey films didn't live up to audience expectations. It didn't help matters that James Cagney's second vehicle for Grand National, *Something to Sing About* (1937), was a costly flop that left Alperson in a financial hole and drove his big-name star back into the waiting arms of the brothers Warner. The company never recouped its considerable investment in Cagney and went belly-up in 1939.

Ultimately, the failures of *The Shadow Strikes* and *International Crime* are attributable to Max and Arthur Alexander, whose refusal to properly fund, cast, and develop the series proved they couldn't see past the end of a balance sheet. Yet it would not have taken a fortune to produce Shadow movies that pleased theatergoers. It would only have taken some respect for the property and the application of common sense. But at every creative crossroad Max and Arthur made the wrong turn. And that became a habit, which explains why they spent the remainder of their careers grinding out bottom-of-the-barrel product for the cheesiest outfits in Hollywood.

For his next big-screen outing the Master of Darkness appeared in a cliffhanger serial that borrowed elements from both the pulp and radio incarnations of the character.

Harry Cohn's Columbia Pictures Corporation was a late player in the serial game, coming to bat in 1937 after various independent producers had departed the field for good. With only Universal and Republic as competition, the studio initially outsourced chapter-play production to the father-son team of Louis and Adrian Weiss, whose Artclass Pictures had long been a mainstay of Poverty Row. Their three serials for Columbia—*Jungle Menace*, *The Mysterious Pilot*, and *The Secret of Treasure Island*—were undistinguished efforts that underperformed in the marketplace. Cohn summarily dismissed Weiss *pere et fils*, assigning newly hired producer Jack Fier to oversee *The Great Adventures of Wild Bill Hickok*, previously announced as the fourth Weiss/Columbia serial of the 1937-38 season.

Fier determined that the only effective way to seize serial market share was to bring Columbia's chapter-play production in house and make the studio's episodic epics on a slightly grander scale than originally contemplated. This, presumably, would make them more appealing to exhibitors previously reliant on Universal and Republic product.

Columbia's four 1938-39 serials—led by *The Spider's Web*, an action-packed adaptation of the Popular Publications hero pulp that was *The*

Shadow Magazine's most serious competitor—enjoyed considerable box-office success but failed to return the expected margin of profit because their production costs were so high. At a time when the average Republic and Universal serial cost $150,000 to $175,000, Fier was spending well over $200,000 for each of his. Since exhibitor rentals at this time averaged five dollars per chapter, the extra expenditures cut into Columbia's revenues.

The somewhat more lavishly appointed Fier-produced chapter plays did, however, secure enough bookings and generate sufficiently favorable publicity to solidify the studio's position in this niche market. But, having accomplished this aim, Harry Cohn retrenched by once again outsourcing serial production, this time to Larry Darmour, who for some years had been supplying Columbia with short subjects and "B"-grade Westerns on an independent basis. Cohn and Fier were gambling that serial production quality was secondary to promotional value: With an exhibitor client base established, they reasoned it would be just as easy to sell the studio's chapter plays based on the presence of marketable stars or popular characters licensed from other mediums.

It fell to Jack Fier to select properties with appeal to the generally youthful audience that patronized serials. This meant obtaining screen rights to characters from pulps, comics, and radio shows. With Darmour hired to produce four chapter plays per "season" (in those days, a movie "season" began sometime after Labor Day and extended through Spring to the beginning of Summer, which typically saw a reduction in theatergoing), Fier commenced his licensing efforts.

The all-important season-opening slot had been reserved for a serial built around some popular fictional character. Following negotiations with Street & Smith, Columbia on May 26, 1939 paid $7,000 for the right to produce one motion picture, either a 15-episode serial or a long feature film, based on The Shadow. Surviving documents reveal that the publishing company's vice president and general manager Henry W. "Bill" Ralston and licensing director William de Grouchy exercised great care in crafting the agreement and insisted the filmmakers maintain fidelity to Street & Smith's most profitable pulp hero.

Significantly, however, the deal permitted Columbia to adapt episodes of the radio show as well as novels printed in the magazine. This was a potentially risky concession because the two versions of The Shadow were fundamentally incompatible. In a July 19 letter to the publishing company, Columbia vice president B. B. Kahane informed Street & Smith that the studio had decided to use as source material "The Green Hoods"

This image of the one-sheet poster for the 1940 Shadow serial is a transparency of Glenn Cravath's original art. The lettering at bottom is a poorly fitted overlay.

(published in the August 15, 1938 issue), "Silver Skull" (January 1, 1939), and "The Lone Tiger" (February 15, 1939). He also requested a copy of the script to one of the radio episodes, "Prelude to Terror" (broadcast January 29, 1939).

Apparently, Fier at first intended to produce the Shadow serial in house. Brief news items published in movie-industry trade papers during the early part of summer reported that Lorna Gray would take the female lead, and that Norman Deming and D. Ross Lederman would direct in tandem. As all were under contract to Columbia, these accounts lend credence to the supposition that the chapter play was initially slated for more extravagant production mounting along the lines of *The Spider's Web*. But when Larry Darmour signed on to supply serials for Columbia distribution the property was assigned to him.

Writers Joseph F. Poland and Ned Dandy, who had collaborated on the previous two Fier-produced serials, teamed with accomplished scripter Joseph O'Donnell to devise a story containing 15 episodes of thrills that could be realized cinematically on short money. (They were assisted by Charles Condon and John Thomas Neville, whose contributions could not have been substantial as they did not receive screen credit.) Reportedly, Darmour's Columbia chapter plays were budgeted at $100,000—less than half what Fier had been spending. Speed and economy became the new watchwords of Columbia's serial unit. Sound-stage scenes would be shot at Larry Darmour's studio on Santa Monica Boulevard in Hollywood. Exterior street scenes would be taken in Burbank at what was called the Columbia Ranch, or on the adjoining Warner Brothers back lot, access to which was available for a modest rental fee. The screenwriters kept cost limitations very much in mind as they concocted the scenario, and by mid-July a first draft had been completed.

Of course, helming the production of action-packed and highly melodramatic serials required a master's touch, so at Fier's suggestion Darmour hired James W. Horne, who had co-directed *The Spider's Web* and *Flying G-Men*. Although Horne was best known for his comedies, including many shorts and features starring Laurel & Hardy, he directed numerous chapter plays in the silent era, among them *Bull's Eye* (1917) and *Hands Up!* (1918), which had made box-office sensations of their respective stars, Eddie Polo and Ruth Roland.

The casting process yielded mixed results, although Darmour scored a coup by landing highly regarded major-studio player Victor Jory for the lead role. Actually, Darmour didn't make the deal himself. Canadian-born

```
           COLUMBIA PICTURES CORPORATION
                   OF CALIFORNIA, LTD.
                  1438 GOWER STREET
                  HOLLYWOOD, CALIFORNIA
                     HOLLYWOOD 3181


                        July 19, 1939



Street & Smith Publications, Inc.
79 Seventh Avenue
New York, N. Y.

Gentlemen:

Reference is hereby made to the Agreement between us, dated
May 26, 1939, whereby we acquired the right to make one serial
motion picture to be based upon any or all of the literary
works mentioned in Schedules "A" and "B" attached to said
Agreement.

Please be advised that we do hereby elect to acquire the
motion picture rights to the following literary works:

                    FROM SCHEDULE "A"
          THE GREEN HOODS - Published August 15, 1938
          SILVER SKULL    -    "      January 1, 1939
          THE LONE TIGER  -    "      February 15, 1939

                    FROM SCHEDULE "B"
          PRELUDE TO TERROR - January 29, 1939

We are giving you this notice in accordance with the provisions
of Article I of the above mentioned Agreement, dated May 26, 1939.

                              Very truly yours,

                              COLUMBIA PICTURES CORPORATION

                              By _____
                                      Vice President
```

Jory had been working for Columbia off and on since 1934, and he enjoyed a good relationship with the notoriously irascible Harry Cohn. Even though the darkly handsome, vaguely sinister-looking actor had played leads before, he found steadier work in character parts and in 1939 was considered one of Hollywood's top heavies. His film work that year had already included high-profile villain portrayals in *Dodge City* and *Gone with the Wind*.

"My agent told me he'd made a two-picture deal for me at Columbia," Jory recalled to me in a 1980 interview. "Harry Cohn threw me into [the serial]. He said, 'Vic, you're going to be The Shadow.' It was as simple as that."

The serial's storyline combined elements of both pulp magazine and radio show, although it naturally leaned toward the former, as contractually obligated. The chief element borrowed from The Shadow's airwave adventures was Margot Lane, played by blonde, brassy Veda Ann Borg, a former Warner Brothers starlet most frequently seen as a gangster's moll or wisecracking showgirl. Borg lost her berth at Warners following a car accident in which she suffered serious facial injuries after being thrown through the windshield. Darmour had used her previously in a Bill Elliott Western, *The Law Comes to Texas* (1939), and she agreed to do the Shadow serial while waiting for another round of plastic surgery. Since she still bore facial scars Veda had to be made up, lit and photographed carefully, so she received very few close-ups. A talented actress, Borg was nonetheless ill suited to play the glamorous, sophisticated Margot of the radio series.

Rounding out the starring trio was one Roger Moore, cast as The Shadow's chief aide, Harry Vincent. Moore was in fact Joe Young, the older brother of second-tier movie star and TV's future Marcus Welby, Robert Young. Joe's career had never really taken off, and the role of Vincent was the last sizable one he got. Although he continued to work well into the Fifties, after *The Shadow* the elder Young most frequently appeared in uncredited bit parts. Also seen as familiar figures from the pulp magazine were veteran character actors Frank LaRue, playing Commissioner Ralph Weston, and Edward Peil, as Inspector Joe Cardona.

Principal photography began in the fall of 1939—the exact date is unknown—and proceeded at a rapid clip. "We did 15 episodes in 30 days," said Jory years later. "Less, actually, because we didn't shoot on Sundays. It was hard work—early mornings, late nights, a lot of rushing around." The Fier-produced serials, by contrast, had consumed six to eight weeks of shooting time.

Horne impressed upon his actors a need for speed and didn't waste time on the niceties of staging scenes. "He instructed us very quickly," Jory remembered. "No real direction in terms of performances, except that we had to take everything 'big.' He'd sketch the where and how of a scene, and give us the basic attitude of it, but mostly it was a question of hitting the marks and delivering the lines on cue. We did damn few retakes, and only then if there had been a problem with camera or sound. On serials you didn't get multiple takes to experiment with different line readings."

Lamont Cranston in his Lin Chang role (Victor Jory, left) takes a warning from Wu Yung (Philip Ahn) while Harry Vincent (Joe Young) listens intently.

While shooting *The Shadow*, Horne introduced another time-saving innovation to shave hours off the schedule. In those days, fight scenes were always shot twice—once in a "master" shot that took in the whole set and covered the melee from beginning to end, then with a series of shorter, closer shots that sometimes showed the principals throwing punches, rather than their stunt doubles. These "insert" shots would be cut into the masters to quicken the sequence's pace and further the illusion that the actors were doing their own fighting.

George DeNormand, an experienced stuntman who doubled Victor Jory in *The Shadow*, explained to me in 1973 that Horne came up with a way to avoid the time-consuming process of relighting the set for close-ups and refitting it with duplicates of props that had been damaged or destroyed in the first take. "Instead of shooting the scene twice," said DeNormand, "[Horne] got actors who could do their own fights and used them as the heavies. Then he set up two cameras, side by side. One camera took the master shot from a fixed position. The other was tricked out with a special lens that would give you a closer view. The second operator was told to follow me around the set [by swiveling the camera]. This way, the director could chop up the second-camera footage to get those quick, close cuts he needed to edit into the master shot, without having to set everything up a second time. There was never a worry I'd be recognized in the closer view because I was wearing the hat and the cape and a little strip mask that covered the bottom half of my face."

Horne used this technique sparingly in *The Shadow* but more extensively in the following nine Columbia chapter plays he directed for Larry Darmour. (For the subsequent serials DeNormand was replaced as lead double by Eddie Parker and, in the Western cliffhangers, by Cliff Lyons.)

Margot (Veda Ann Borg) gets vital instructions from The Shadow as he plans a daring raid on the Black Tiger's henchmen, hard at work on their master's latest destructive scheme.

Cinematographer James S. Brown Jr. and his assistant "undercranked" fight scenes to speed up the action, making the brawls seem more furious but also giving them a Keystone Kops aspect that latter-day viewers find risible. In a way, though, that was intentional. While directing his Darmour serials Horne never fully sublimated his comedic leanings.

For reasons unknown, *The Shadow* had a national release date of January 5, 1940, several months later than the typical season-opening serial. Street & Smith promoted the film extensively, mentioning it several times in the magazine's "Highlights on The Shadow" department and some of the company's other pulps. The chapter play's theatrical playoff period coincided with an increased effort to exploit the character's commercial potential; 1940 saw the marketing of numerous licensed products and multi-media spin-offs. Fans could buy Shadow hats, masks, cloaks, board games, make-up kits, gun-and-holster sets, and other paraphernalia tangentially connected to the Master of Darkness. Street & Smith launched a Shadow comic book in March of 1940, and a newspaper strip syndicated by the Ledger Syndicate followed shortly thereafter.

Of course, buying a comic book or board game wasn't nearly as exciting as seeing one's favorite character live on the big screen, and Columbia's *Shadow* packed houses with devotees of radio show and pulp magazine alike. Serial fans huddled in darkened theaters all across the country learned in Chapter One, "The Doomed City," that the economic life of a great metropolis was being threatened by a well-organized criminal body headed by a mysterious figure known as the Black Tiger, whose mad ambition was to acquire "supreme financial power." To this end he waged a systematic campaign of terrorization and destruction—blowing up factories, crashing trains and planes, extorting money from fear-paralyzed tycoons.

The serial's villain, the Black Tiger, goes under the ray that renders him invisible, protecting his true identity from the viewer as well as his hapless henchmen.

The city's captains of industry prevailed upon Lamont Cranston (described as a "noted scientist and criminologist") to help combat the Tiger and his minions. Unbeknownst to them, Cranston had created two separate personalities to further his fight against crime: Lin Chang, a shifty Chinese merchant with underworld ties, and The Shadow, a mystery man whose hat, cloak, and sinister laugh were trademarks instantly recognizable to evildoers everywhere.

The Black Tiger's identity was a closely guarded secret: Not even his own men know who the Tiger really was, because he possessed the power of invisibility and transmitted instructions to the gang, sight unseen, through a wood-mounted tiger head outfitted with glowing eyes and radio speaker. But as the serial progressed it became apparent that he was one of the industrialists who met regularly with Cranston and Commissioner Weston at the Cobalt Club.

Week after week, The Shadow fought the Black Tiger to a standstill, nearly losing his life at the close of each episode only to escape miraculously at the beginning of the next. The chapter-ending perils lacked ingenuity; an inordinate number of installments closed with a ceiling collapsing on the fallen, unconscious Shadow—who groggily disengaged himself from the wreckage and staggered away the following week.

Truth be told, *The Shadow* didn't follow the pulp magazine or radio show as closely as it did *The Spider's Web*. In fact, it's fair to assume that screenwriters Dandy, Poland, and O'Donnell were instructed to copy the earlier serial, a box-office smash that single-handedly made Columbia a force to reckon with in the chapter-play market. The similarities are marked: *The Shadow*'s Lamont Cranston, like *Web*'s Richard Wentworth, is identified as a scientific criminologist rather than as the wealthy dilettante and world

Once seated behind his desk, the Black Tiger speaks through this electrified tiger-head model outfitted with a radio loudspeaker.

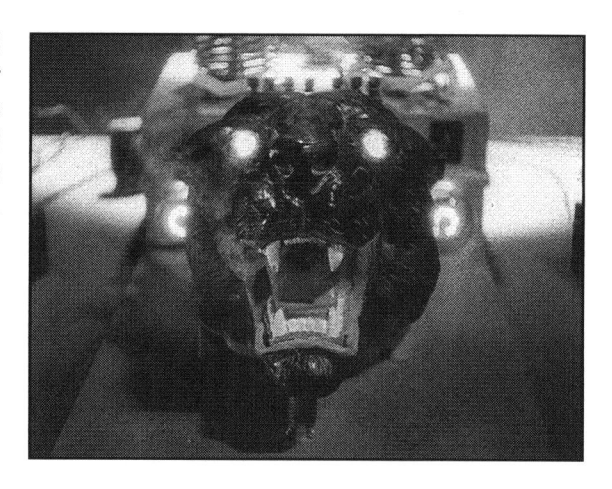

traveler he is in Walter Gibson's stories. The Lin Chang identity corresponds with no character in the Shadow saga but performs the same narrative function as Wentworth's Blinky McQuade persona. Likewise, the serial's Harry Vincent doesn't act independently, as he generally does in the pulp yarns; he stays close to The Shadow in the manner of Wentworth's aides Jackson and Ram Singh.

Moreover, *The Shadow* utilizes the same basic plot as *The Spider's Web*. Both serials posit the existence of a deranged mastermind who employs an army of henchmen to terrorize industrial leaders in a bid for economic control of a major city. Both show the police powerless to stem the tide of terror resulting from heedless destruction of life and property, concentrated on modes of transportation and newly invented devices.

The writers didn't entirely ignore the Shadow of pulp and radio. The serial is littered with bits and pieces of the licensed material. For example, the master villain's name and a courtroom scene in Chapter One are clearly inspired by "The Lone Tiger." The opening installment's climax, in which exploding light bulbs (!) are set off by a sudden surge of current, is adapted from "Prelude to Terror." A Chapter Two sequence, in which a disguised Shadow enters the Black Tiger's lair by donning one of the full-face masks worn by the villain's henchmen during meetings with their leader, was clearly inspired by a similar episode in "The Green Hoods."

The chapter play's scripters mined several plot nuggets from "Silver Skull." For example, one scene from that novel finds The Shadow trapped in an underground chamber and taunted by the mystery villain, who speaks through a life-sized mechanical skull outfitted with a radio speaker. While taunting his enemy, Silver Skull fills the room with gas—which, ignited by sparks, causes an explosion that brings the roof crashing down on The

Glenn Cravath did this watercolor "rough" for a large canvas banner that would hang in front of theaters playing the serial, usually under their marquees.

Shadow, who narrowly escapes. Poland, Dandy, and O'Donnell got two cliffhanger endings out of that one Walter Gibson-devised incident. Other "Silver Skull" elements employed in *The Shadow* include the systematic kidnapping of wealthy and powerful men and the repeated destruction of airplanes by mysterious means.

Aside from Margot's presence and the aforementioned bit with the exploding light bulbs, the serial took nothing from the Shadow radio show. Darmour and company made a reasonable effort to ensure that followers of the pulp Shadow would recognize their hero on screen. (In this respect, it should be noted, the serial improved on *The Shadow Strikes* and *International Crime*, those dismal 1937-38 feature films starring Rod La Rocque.) However, several minor but jarring differences could be noted. Harry Vincent shuttles The Shadow to and from most of his confrontations with the Black Tiger's men. Sometimes, however, he is shown driving a taxicab and wearing a hack's cap. This suggests that the pulp Shadow's usual driver, cabbie Moe Shrevnitz, was originally included in the script, only to have his character combined with that of Vincent for cost-cutting purposes. Also, despite Street & Smith's insistence that the serial Shadow deploy his trademark automatic pistols, he uses automatics and .38-caliber revolvers interchangeably.

These inconsistencies are puzzling because Street & Smith had specifically requested changes to the first-draft script forwarded to them by Columbia. A July 21 letter from the studio's F. L. Weber to Bill Ralston acknowledged receipt of a Street & Smith memo expressing concerns about scenario deviations from Shadow lore. After expressing gratitude for cooperation extended to the serial's writers by Walter Gibson and *Shadow Magazine* editor John Nanovic, Weber assured Ralston that numerous minor

Margot (Veda Ann Borg) is menaced by Black Tiger henchman Flint (Jack Ingram), but The Shadow (Victor Jory) comes to her aid in this studio-shot publicity photo.

but significant corrections would be made based on their input. "The Shadow's guns will definitely be two .45 automatics, as requested," wrote the Columbia executive. That promise went unfulfilled.

Weber also addressed the fact that Harry Vincent was occasionally seen driving a cab in usurpation of Moe Shrevnitz's function in the novels. "As regards Harry Vincent," he explained, "we are not using the character of Moe Shrevnitz. We will place a line in the first episode stating that Harry is filling in for Shrevnitz, due to his illness." Another note stated: "As regards Burbank, we are changing this character, so it will be Richards playing the role of the manservant." Both characters were regulars in the pulp yarns, but neither turned up in the Columbia chapter play, suggesting that cost-conscious Darmour had second thoughts about including them after script revisions had been made. Other alterations requested by Street & Smith including changing the screenwriters' Metropolitan Club to the Cobalt Club and making Cranston an independent research scientist with his own lab, rather than an employee of Stanford Marshall, one of the industrialists targeted by the Black Tiger.

One of the goofier publicity photos released to help promote The Shadow, this shot features ex-wrestler Constantine Romanoff, a favorite of director James W. Horne.

Nonetheless, The Shadow fared better in his one and only chapter play than many characters adapted from other media. Spy Smasher, for example, gained a twin brother. Blackhawk lost two of his subordinates. And Captain Marvel suffered the ignominious loss of his powers in the final chapter of *his* serial. All things considered, the Master of Darkness could have done a lot worse.

Victor Jory deserves the lion's share of credit for the serial's effectiveness. His features don't exactly match those described by Gibson as belonging to Cranston, but they come pretty close. He projects confidence and authority in the role, and it's hard not to appreciate his approximation of The Shadow's trademark laugh. "Oh, I had to get that right," Jory recalled in 1980. "*Everybody* knew that laugh, even people who didn't listen to the radio show every Sunday afternoon. It was a thing, you know, kind of like a catch phrase. 'The Shadow knows' was a popular saying. Comedians on the radio joked about it. So I practiced that chuckle until I felt I had it right. You wanted it to give the kids goose bumps; that was the idea."

Harry Vincent (Joe Young, billed as Roger Moore) stands guard as The Shadow makes a quick change to his Lin Chang persona under the watchful eye of Wu Yung (Philip Ahn), owner of the Oriental Bazaar.

James W. Horne's deliberately arch directorial style makes it difficult for today's viewers to appreciate *The Shadow*, which Columbia TriStar Home Video released on VHS cassettes in 1997. The combination of overacting, undercranking, and what film historian William K. Everson called "moments of truly lunatic comedy involving the villains" irritates serial buffs used to the more serious chapter plays of other studios. (Hard-core devotees take particular umbrage at a scene in which one of the Tiger's henchmen implores another, "Tell me the story of Red Riding Hood again. I like that one.") But Everson, in his introduction to Alan G. Barbour's 1970 history of serials, *Days of Thrills and Adventure*, probably got it right: "[Horne] was too good a director, too much a past master of great silent and sound comedy, not to know precisely what he was doing. Undoubtedly he reasoned that to play the scripts straight, with their stereotyped stories and meager budgets, could only result in serials spectacularly inferior to the competitive ones issued by Republic and Universal. Playing them for comedy didn't make them better, but it did keep them lively, distinctive, and different."

Actually, of the ten Columbia chapter plays James Horne made for producer Larry Darmour before dying in 1942, *The Shadow* contains the fewest cringeworthy moments of campy humor. Unlike *The Green Archer* (1940) and *The Iron Claw* (1941), to name just two, the serial generally preserves its main character's dignity. It surely could have been more faithful to the source material, but *The Shadow* has a lot more going for it than the character's other big-screen incarnations.

In his interview with me, Victor Jory stated: "I've been in a lot of good films and worked with many of the best stars, writers and directors in the business. But, you know, I'd have to say that more people know me from *The Shadow* than anything else I've done. I still get fan mail mentioning it.

Jory and this author in 1980, flanked by fans Richard W. Bann (L) and Joe Judice.

Here [at the Charlotte Western Film Fair] I've had probably a dozen people come up to me and ask me to do the laugh. It's the damnedest thing."

The Shadow was followed by three more 1940 Columbia serials adapted from properties created for other media: *Terry and the Pirates* (based on Milton Caniff's popular comic strip), *Deadwood Dick* (updating a venerable character of late-19th century dime novels), and *The Green Archer* (from Edgar Wallace's celebrated mystery novel, previously turned into a wildly successful serial by Pathé in 1925). If one is to believe exhibitor reports published in the trade journal *Motion Picture Herald*, the Shadow serial was the most popular of the quartet. But apparently not so much as to induce Columbia to produce a sequel, especially since the contract with Street & Smith called for a bump in the licensing fee to $8,500 should the studio want to revisit the character.

The Shadow as a big-screen property took an enforced hiatus of six years, finally materializing as the star of three low-budget feature films.

The June 2, 1945 issue of *Motion Picture Herald*, one of the movie industry's leading trade papers, reported on the annual board of directors meeting of Monogram Pictures Corporation in Chicago. At this gathering, chairman of the board W. Ray Johnston announced a slate of 43 feature films to be produced for the 1945-46 theatrical season beginning that fall. Among the series offerings greenlighted for production were three Charlie Chan mysteries, four East Side Kids comedies, and two "chillers" that were to feature The Shadow.

Monogram had recently licensed screen rights to pulpdom's Master of Darkness, who for all his success in pulps and on radio had not made much impression on moviegoers. The Shadow was originally intended for erstwhile Poverty Row filmmaker A. W. Hackel, at that time making "B" pictures on a cost-plus basis for Monogram release. But without warning the studio assigned the property to newly minted producer Joe Kaufman, a 34-year-old former executive with the Balaban & Katz theater circuit. His first film, *Sensation Hunters* (1945), had just been released and was doing pretty good business. He was deemed a young man with a future.

Kaufman assembled a production unit from the ranks of salaried Monogram employees and freelance technicians who frequently hired out for work on inexpensive "B" pictures. Director Phil Rosen and screenwriter George Callahan had worked in tandem on Monogram's Charlie Chan films and were logical choices for the Shadow series. Production manager Glenn Cook and assistant director Eddie Davis had been on the studio payroll for years, along with musical director Edward Kay, sound recordist Tom Lambert, and art directors Dave Milton and E. R. "Ernie" Hickson. Head cinematographer William Sickner and film editor Ace Herman were relative newcomers to the studio but had worked on "B" pictures and serials at Universal for most of the sound era.

While no cost sheets from the company's Shadow movies seem to exist, available numbers from comparable Monogram films suggest that Kaufman's per-picture budget was probably in the $40,000-50,000 range. Working closely with associate producer Lou Brock and scripter Callahan, he devised a story that utilized several standing sets for interiors. The few exterior scenes would be filmed on the Monogram lot, with one side of the studio's administration building standing in for a warehouse.

Handsome, square-jawed Kane Richmond was cast as Lamont Cranston. No stranger to pulp-ish story material, he had recently scored in several popular movie serials: *Spy Smasher* (1942), *Haunted Harbor* (1944), *Jungle Raiders* and *Brenda Starr, Reporter* (both 1945). Barbara Read, one of Universal's original Three Smart Girls, took the role of Margo Lane. Former stage comedian and venerable character actor Tom Dugan signed on to play Shrevvy (the spelling of whose nickname was inexplicably changed to Shrevvie), who doubled as Cranston's butler and the driver of his privately owned cab. The part of Police Commissioner Weston went to Pierre Watkin, and short, stocky Joseph Crehan portrayed Inspector Joe Cardona. Minor day-players were cast as Shadow agents Burbank and Hawkeye, who appeared together in a short sequence near the film's beginning.

This re-issue poster shows Monogram's Shadow sans his face-covering mask.

It should be noted at this point that Monogram's Shadow films took little to nothing from the character's radio incarnation, preferring instead to rely for inspiration on Walter B. Gibson's pulp stories, which by this time had degenerated into formulaic whodunits not unlike the studio's Charlie Chan films. Indeed, George Callahan's script for the series opener could very well have been a rewritten Chan opus, with Margo substituting for Charlie's Number Three Son Tommy and Shrevvie for Chan's chauffeur Birmingham Brown. Callahan made Cranston the nephew of Commissioner Weston and an amateur criminologist whose insistence on joining his uncle at crime scenes irritated the blustery Cardona no end.

What was originally titled *The Shadow* went before the cameras in late October 1945 and took two weeks to complete. It was retitled *The Shadow Returns* during the editing process and scheduled for national release on February 16, 1946, with preview screenings for trade-paper critics taking place in January. The notices were mixed, with even the positive ones more polite than enthusiastic.

Motion Picture Herald's anonymous scribe scored the picture as "Good" and in the body of the notice called it "a better-than-average melodrama," singling out Richmond and Reed for praise.

Thalia Bell, reviewing the picture for *Motion Picture Daily*, was nothing if not generous. "The first of Monogram's new series of melodramas, based on the radio program The Shadow [sic], is acceptable in its category. Within the limits of his budget, Joe Kaufman has given the film adequate production, and director Phil Rosen, an old-timer in the field of melodrama, keeps matters moving at a breakneck pace. [!] Kane Richmond is outstanding in a dual role. Barbara Reed is charming as the Shadow's girl friend."

Harrison's Reports: "First in Monogram's new 'Shadow' series, there is not much to recommend it, for the story is confusing and developed mostly by dialogue, causing one to lose interest in the proceedings. To some extent it attempts to follow the formula of the 'Thin Man' pictures by having the hero's sweetheart help solve the crime, but the plot development are so lacking in freshness and the comedy is so labored that it fails to be either interesting or amusing. Whatever excitement the melodramatic action may create is rendered ineffectual by the silly comic interpolations. Even the performances are only fair; but this is probably due to the fact that the players were unable to cope with the mediocre material, as well as with the uninspired direction."

The story begins on an eerie note. One dark night, just as Lamont Cranston (Richmond) promises his fiancée, Margo Lane (Reed), that he'll

Kane Richmond and Barbara Read played Lamont and Margo as though they were low-budget simulacrums of The Thin Man*'s Nick and Nora Charles, with an unfortunate emphasis on Margo's flightiness.*

give up sleuthing and schedule their wedding in three weeks if a good case doesn't come along, a detective from the Burbank Agency encourages him to observe that night's proceedings at Forest Park Cemetery: A bearded, fidgety man named Josef Yomans is unearthing a pouch of jewels from a coffin. Police commissioner J. R. Weston (Watkin), Lamont's uncle, is also notified and sends Inspector Joe Cardona (Crehan) to investigate.

When Yomans mysteriously disappears after securing the pouch, Cardona and Lamont follow his trail to the house of eccentric tycoon Michael Hasdon (Frank Reicher), true owner of the jewels. Also awaiting Yomans at Hasdon's is a syndicate formed to buy the gems. Cardona interrogates the group, which consists of importer-exporter Charles Frobay (Robert Emmett Keane), ex-racketeer William Monk (Lester Dorr), former showgirl Lenore Jessup (Rebel Randall), and timid, myopic businessman Robert Buell (Sherry Hall). Also present are Hasdon's secretary Paul Breck (Emmett Vogan) and butler John Adams (Cyril Delevanti).

The eccentric businessman registers indignance, stalks out the room, and marches upstairs. Donning his Shadow disguise of black hat, mask, and trench coat, Lamont follows and corners the tycoon in a room with French doors opening on a balcony. Suddenly Hasdon pitches over the rail and breaks his neck falling to the patio below. His death is preliminarily ruled a suicide and Cardona leaves the house after warning the other inhabitants to stay in town until an investigation can be completed.

After leaving the house with Cardona, Lamont doubles back, again garbed as The Shadow, eavesdrops on the group. The syndicate's members persuade Breck to help them drive Frobay, who has also left the house, from their syndicate.

Lamont and Margo are driven to Frobay's warehouse by Cranston's valet and chauffeur Shrevvie (Dugan). After observing Hasdon's butler Adams sneaking into the building, they follow and are stopped by a guard, who ushers them to Frobay's office to give an accounting of themselves. Cranston informs Frobay that his confederates are plotting against him. While the importer's back is turned, Lamont rifles through his desk drawer and extracts a gemstone and a small notebook. Frobay allows his unwanted guests to leave unmolested, but upon returning to his car Lamont finds a dead body in the back seat. The unidentified victim is summarily delivered to police headquarters. By virtue of his relation to Weston, Lamont is not suspected—but Cardona wonders about the playboy's connection to the Hasdon affair.

Back at his Broadmoor Arms apartment, Cranston examines the pilfered gem and guesses that it is not a jewel at all. As he leafs through Frobay's notebook, which contains several chemical formulas, Burbank calls to report that no duty was levied on Hasdon's gems, thus proving they are not precious stones.

When Cardona reconvenes the group at Hasdon's that evening, The Shadow, attends and knocks Adams unconscious when the butler acts suspiciously outside the second-floor room with the balcony. He then calls to Cardona and importunes the inspector to question Adams. But when Cardona goes upstairs and approaches Adams, the butler plunges over the same balcony to certain death—another apparent suicide.

Once again disguised as The Shadow, Lamont has Shrevvie drive him back to the warehouse. As he interrogates Frobay, the importer suddenly falls over the side of the tall wooden staircase to his office high above the warehouse floor. The Shadow and his bumbling agent narrowly escape, and only after engaging several of the importer's employees in a fistfight.

Subsequently the corpse found in Lamont's car is identified as Yomans. Cranston decides that someone posed as Yomans to obtain the jewels and spirit them to Hasdon's house before the impersonation could be discovered. Pressing his luck, Lamont and Margo return to the warehouse—now under police guard—and persuade the officer at the door that they have come with Cardona's blessings to continue the investigation. Finding a hidden laboratory behind a secret door in a large packing case, Lamont spies

A warehouse guard (unidentified player) brings Shrevvie (Tom Dugan), Margo (Barbara Reed) and Lamont (Kane Richmond) to Frobay (Robert Emmett Keane).

a wall safe and removes the other missing jewels. Having deduced that the formulas in Frobay's notebook hold the key to the mystery, Cranston mixes the chemical solution and, on a hunch, dumps the jewels into this soup. The so-called gems dissolve, releasing steel capsules in which he finds pieces of microfilm containing parts of another formula—one for a super-strong plastic, which is what the Hasdon "jewels" were made of. Obviously, this multi-million-dollar formula provides a powerful motive for murder.

After summoning Weston and Cardona and reassembling the group of suspects at Hasdon's house, Lamont plants the formula in his uncle's pocket. He then directs Cardona's attention to the many bullwhips that adorn Hasdon's walls—souvenirs of his world travels. The inspector finally tumbles to what Cranston had already guessed: that the killer used whips to seize his victims' wrists from below and drag them over the rails. Lamont also shows how the murderer could have used the door to a connecting room to gain the hallway unseen and then rejoin the group after pulling Hasdon and Adams to their deaths. Breck, the only suspect known to be proficient with a bullwhip, makes a break by charging to the stairs from the hallway. Cranston flicks the whip around the secretary's arm and yanks him tumbling down the stairs. It is also revealed that Breck impersonated Yomans the night he exhumed the coffin and took the jewels. Joe Cardona grudgingly acknowledges Lamont's contribution to the case's solving.

Callahan's unnecessarily complicated plot is full of holes, and the film leaves many questions unanswered. Why were the fake jewels smuggled into the country in a coffin? What was Josef Yomans' role in the scheme? Why did Breck impersonate Yomans at all, knowing that he planned to kill the man once he'd obtained the jewels? How did Breck learn that Cranston went to Frobay's warehouse to interrogate the impostor? (Remember, he also entered the warehouse and killed Frobay before The Shadow's eyes.) What was the point of dumping Yomans' body into Cranston's cab, knowing that Weston's cousin would easily evade suspicion?

Any director would have been hard-pressed to make an effective mystery from George Callahan's half-baked script, which also contained a surfeit of corny gags and nonsensical dialogue. Tom Dugan's Shrevvie got the most moronic lines, some of them delivered so off-handedly that they smacked of improvisation. In one scene he leaves Lamont and Margo in the apartment to make a raft of sandwiches, only to be caught holding them in an empty room when the couple charges off to follow a newly discovered clue. "Now what am I going to do with these sandwiches?" Shrevvie asks himself out loud. Suddenly his eyes light up. "I know what I'm going to do with them. I'm going to eat them myself. It's a dandy idea!"

Yet *The Shadow Returns* was not without interest, and if a viewer didn't compare it too closely to one of Walter B. Gibson's novels (which themselves weren't any too good at this period in *Shadow Magazine* history) he would be entertained. The Shadow's entrance in every scene is heralded by a memorably eerie piece of music—likely composed by musical director Edward Kay—that's heavy on organ, which makes it reminiscent of an old-time radio melodrama. Even more impressive is the character's visualization as, well, a shadow, appearing on walls, the panels of doors, and the sides of buildings. The use of silhouette is frequently creative, redounding to the credit of cinematographer William Sicker, who obviously spent extra time lighting sets to achieve the desired effect.

It's often possible to gauge the popularity of a film by reading the contemporaneous reports of exhibitors who commented on the new releases in such well-read trade-paper columns as the *Motion Picture Herald*'s "What the Picture Did for Me." By opining on the pictures and their box-office performances, theater men often influenced their brethren to either embrace or shun current product. Strangely, I could not find a single exhibitor comment on *Shadow Returns* in any of the *Herald*'s weekly issues for 1946.

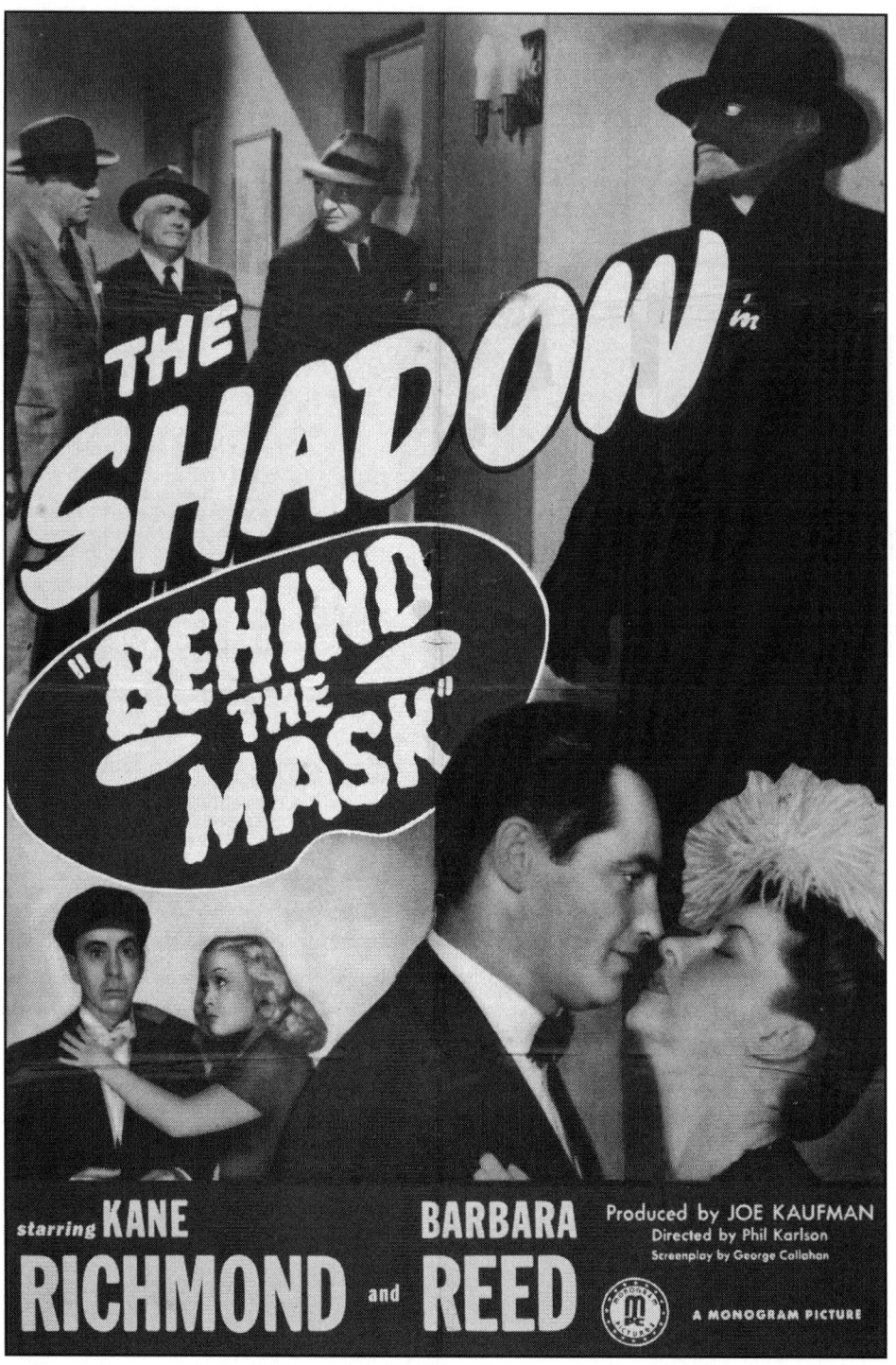

Monogram's second Shadow film took a turn for the worse, adding Dorothea Kent to the cast as Margo's scatterbrained maid and inserting too much comedy.

Character actor George Chandler (left) replaced Tom Dugan as Shrevvie in *Behind the Mask,* but the emphasis on comedy rendered the substitution meaningless.

Variety reviewed major-studio "A" films after trade screenings but often critiqued "B" movies after seeing them in theaters with average audiences. The industry's leading trade paper didn't get around to reviewing *The Shadow Returns* until August, and it was none too generous in its appraisal. The critic led his notice with three words: "An unexciting whodunit." He had seen the film as the bottom half of a double bill at Brooklyn's Strand theater, where he was not the only one underwhelmed: "Plot, on the whole, was accorded frequent yawns by the audience when caught. Richmond, as The Shadow, acquits himself as best he can under circumstances; Barbara Reed, his girl Friday, is on hand mostly for decorative purposes, while Tom Dugan contributes fair comedy relief as The Shadow's chauffeur. Joseph Crehan is an okay inspector.

"Production values are in keeping with the meager budget. Phil Rosen directed at a standard pace and George Callahan's original screenplay faithfully followed the clichés present in similar minor whodunits."

The series' second installment, on which production commenced in late January, was initially titled *The Shadow's Shadow,* although its plot bore

L to R: Weston (Pierre Watkin), Lamont (Kane Richmond), Cardona (Joe Crehan).

no resemblance to the 1933 pulp novel of the same title and was another original Callahan concoction. Principal photography wrapped in early February; the picture was brought in on a two-week schedule, its title changed to *Behind the Mask*. Occupying the director's chair was Phil Karlson (born Phil Karlstein), former Universal prop man and assistant director, who joined Monogram in 1944 and had already helmed seven features—including two Charlie Chans—before accepting the Shadow assignment. He would eventually be recognized as a superb director of *film noir* crime dramas such as the well-regarded *Kansas City Confidential* (1952), *99 River Street* (1953), *The Phenix City Story* (1955), *The Brothers Rico* (1957), and the two-hour pilot for the *Untouchables* TV series, released theatrically as *The Scarface Mob* (1959). Notwithstanding the tight schedule and meager resources allotted to him by producer Joe Kaufman, Karlson took Callahan's script seriously and did his best to make a credible mystery with sharp edges. After suffering ptomaine poisoning during production he was briefly replaced by Monogram contract director William Beaudine, a silent-era veteran reduced to megging Bela Lugosi chillers and East Side Kids comedies for legendarily cheap producer Sam Katzman. Beaudine's contribution to

Shrevvie accompanies The Shadow to a gym in this scene from *Behind the Mask*, but it's a cinch they aren't there for a workout. Monogram's second Shadow movie is the worst of the three.

Kaufmann's second Shadow film has not been established—but then, as a workmanlike journeyman, his style was invisible anyway.

The Shadow Returns was nothing if not a traditional whodunit (albeit a sloppily constructed one), set largely in a huge mansion owned by an eccentric millionaire and populated by suspects engaged in questionable conduct. As previously noted, George Callahan could easily have rewritten one of his Charlie Chan scripts for Kaufman's first Shadow picture. *Behind the Mask* took a slightly different tack, adopting some of the *noir*-ish, hard-boiled trappings of recent "A" thrillers like *Phantom Lady* and *The Big Sleep*. The brightly lit, hermetically sealed crime scene was replaced by seedy nightclubs, dimly lit diners, and rain-soaked streets. This was the milieu of sleazy private eyes, cheap-suited hoods, and bottle-blonde floozies.

Mask's plot revolves around Lamont Cranston's efforts to clear his alter-ego's name after The Shadow is blamed for killing *Daily Bulletin* reporter Jeff Mann (James Cardwell), who's been blackmailing racketeers after collecting evidence against them and threatening to publish it in his newspaper. Among the victims of Mann's shakedowns are Marty Greane (Lou Crosby), a habitué of the Paradise Club, and bookie Mae Bishop (Marjorie Hoshelle), who operates a numbers racket from the Winter Garden.

Cranston persuades Mann's secretary, Edie Merrill (June Clyde), to give him the keys to Mann's apartment, where the newshawk kept his personal files. Then she too is killed under mysterious circumstances. Matters take a silly turn when the jealous Margo (Reed) disguises herself in Shadow garb, slips into Mann's apartment, and is beaten up by an unknown assailant. The murderer is ultimately revealed as *Bulletin* reporter Brad Thomas, Mann's silent partner, who killed his confederate to keep all the blackmail

Frame capture of the main title card for *Behind the Mask*. Monogram's Shadow films were staples of early television, reaching the small screen just a few years after their theatrical playoffs.

money and forestall a double-cross. Cranston tells Inspector Cardona that Thomas used as his murder weapon an empty hypodermic needle, which he used to inject air bubbles into the veins of his victims.

Instead of tamping down the comedy element, Callahan in his screenplay for *Mask* ratcheted up the silliness by giving Shrevvie a dumb-blonde girlfriend named Jennie Delaney (played by Dorothea Kent, who made a specialty of such roles). Tom Dugan was replaced by George Chandler, who portrayed Cranston's butler and driver as somewhat less blockheaded. The addition of Jennie to the roster of principals gave Margo a foil with whom she could plot her own ridiculously intrusive exploits. Whatever suspense was created by the *noir*-ish interludes dissipated rapidly once large chunks of footage were given over to comedy.

Director Karlson and cameraman Sickner collaborated effectively on shots depicting the Master of Darkness as a disembodied shadow. If anything, they paid more attention to this visual device than had *Shadow Returns* director Phil Rosen. In fact, *Mask* is generally a better-looking film than its predecessor, with every penny of its meager budget showing up on screen.

Unfortunately, most reviewers—in both the trade and consumer press—turned thumbs down on *Behind the Mask*, which was released on May 25. *Motion Picture Herald*, which had been kind to *Shadow Returns*, judged *Mask* to be "Poor" and wasted no time pinpointing the reason: "In the latest of Monogram's new Shadow series, Joe Kaufman, producer, and Phil Karlson, director, set out to accomplish that most difficult achievement: a picture at once melodramatic and comic. They missed the mark. Throughout the film, the comedy interferes with the melodrama, and the melodrama negates the comedy." This appraisal was shared by the majority of critics.

Kane Richmond, Dorothea Kent, and George Chandler relax between takes.

For reasons not clear, Monogram asked producer Kaufman to turn out a third Shadow opus for release in August, at the tail end of the 1945-46 season. The most likely explanation is that another producer's film was canceled and a substitution required to meet commitments to exhibitors who had pre-paid for a block of pictures, as was common at that time.

In mid-April the third film went into production as *The Jade Lady*. In addition to writing the script, George Callahan replaced Lou Block as associate producer. Phil Karlson returned to wield the megaphone. Sixty-two-year-old Joseph Crehan took ill at the very beginning of principal photography, and character actor James Flavin—an old hand at playing blustery policemen—replaced him as Cardona. Otherwise, there were no serious complications and shooting was completed within the three-week schedule as planned.

Later retitled *The Missing Lady*, Monogram's third and final Shadow entry proved just as uneven as the first two, with occasional clever touches lost amidst typical Callahan plot complications and protracted episodes of alleged comedy.

Famous curio collector James Douglas (George Lessey) is murdered and his prized possession, a jade statuette said to be worth a quarter of a

63

million dollars, stolen by party or parties unknown. Lamont Cranston investigates the killing and learns that numerous people covet the missing jade lady. Crooked antique dealer Alfred Kester (Douglas Wood) thinks it's in the custody of femme fatale Rose Dawson (Claire Carleton), who is also approached by brutish thug Ox Welsh (Jack Overman) and suavely sinister Terry Blake (James Cardwell).

Adding to the general confusion, Lamont hears a scream issuing from a neighboring apartment at the Broadmoor Arms, where he lives. Upon breaking into the flat and discovering an unconscious woman on the floor near a dead man, he's knocked out. He revives under the ministrations of painter's model Gilda Marsh (Jo Carroll Dennison), who identifies the senseless woman as her sister Anne and the dead man as Alfred Kester.

Subsequently, Anne Marsh accuses Cranston of murdering Kester, and the playboy criminologist is released by his uncle, Commissioner Weston, after being briefly jailed. Artist Jon Field (George J. Lewis), another Broadmoor Arms resident, is entertaining Gilda when Ox Welsh demands that she give him the jade lady—or else. The model plays dumb, and later that night her sister Anne is found murdered shortly after being visited by The Shadow.

This frame capture from *Missing Lady* shows the shadow effect that consumed lots of production time to arrange. But director Karlson and cinematographer Sickner deserve credit for making the extra effort.

A gathering of suspects produces testimony that several of them conspired to steal the jade lady, which is found in a funeral urn in Field's apartment. Terry Blake is revealed to be an insurance investigator; Ox is discovered to have killed Douglas and stolen the statuette at Field's urging; and Gilda Marsh is fingered as the killer of Kester and her own sister, who was secretly married to Ox and planned to double-cross her.

The Missing Lady is the most gritty and violent of the trio, but once again Callahan undercuts the film's impact with unnecessarily confusing plot points and intrusive comedic passages involving Margo, Shrevvie, and Jennie. The Shadow has less screen time than in the previous two series entries, but his appearances are extremely well handled. *Lady* boasts the most impressive of the shadow-on-the-wall effects: a long shot that shows the Dark Avenger climbing a long flight of stairs in silhouette. (See frame enlargement above.)

Today that image would be created by digitally inserting a Shadow whose movements had been captured by rotoscoping. Back in low-tech 1946, Phil Karlson and Bill Sickner accomplished the trick simply and without great expense. The "wall" against which the shadow appeared was actually a large sheet of canvas (maybe several sheets stitched together) stretched taut and nailed to a wooden frame. The staircase, supposedly leading to a second-floor balcony, was placed next to the canvas sheet. On the other side was placed an identically constructed staircase, flush with the one visible to Sickner's camera. Kane Richmond's double, wearing Shadow garb, was lit from an angle to outline his figure in silhouette as he climbed the stairs. The camera captured this movement from the other side of the canvas, from far enough away to create the illusion of a disembodied wraith. It may well have

Another example of the shadow effect used so effectively in *The Missing Lady*. Frances Robinson is the glamour girl getting a grilling from The Shadow.

been the high point of the series, a trick of which even amateur magician Walter Gibson approved.

Reviews were expectedly mixed and tilted negative. *Film Daily* dubbed *Lady* "an interesting whodunit, injected with plenty of brawny treatment." The reviewer added: "Richmond takes a lot of cuffing and dishes it out as well. There is plenty of rough stuff to warm the cockles of those who like this kind of action."

The rival *Motion Picture Daily* expressed a similar opinion: "Customers who prefer their murder mysteries action-packed rather than broadly conversational, and exciting rather than largely suspenseful, will find *The Missing Lady* quite to their liking. It is a film mainly for the neighborhood trade, and the exhibitor who has his patrons' tastes pretty well indexed can rely on the foregoing 'capsule' [appraisal] in determining this one's place in his schedule."

Harrison's Reports, the most brutally frank of the industry sheets, pulled no punches: "Like the previous pictures in the 'Shadow' series, this one is just a minor program mystery-melodrama, handicapped by a story that is so far-fetched and confusing that one loses interest in the proceedings long before the outcome. Considerable stress is placed on the comedy, but most of this is forced and so inane that it is more boring than amusing. The best thing that can be said for it is that on occasion the action is exciting, but it is not enough to sustain one's interest. The players do their best, but they are up against such poor material that their struggle is a hopeless one."

Monogram's Shadow series failed to excite motion-picture audiences despite the character's potent popularity in other media: pulp magazines, radio drama, comic books. The studio made no attempt to renew its license

Kane Richmond in 1962, pointing to a magazine picture of himself as The Shadow.

with Street & Smith. Joe Kaufman got a promotion of sorts, being assigned to a newly created production unit headed by prominent director Roy Del Ruth. Their first film together, *It Happened on Fifth Avenue* (1947), was the initial release of Monogram's subsidiary, Allied Artists Productions. Phil Karlson graduated to better pictures as well, beginning with another 1947 Allied Artists release, the Cinecolor *Black Gold*, starring Anthony Quinn and Katherine De Mille. George Callahan finally escaped the "B" ghetto as well, being relieved of his Charlie Chan duties; Joe Kaufman hired him to write one of the Roy Del Ruth productions, *The Babe Ruth Story* (1948), and as Edward G. O'Callaghan he penned the screenplays for such '50s cult favorites as *This Island Earth*, *Flight to Hong Kong*, and *War of the Planets* before finishing his career writing episodes of various minor TV series.

Kane Richmond's career was already on the wane when he accepted the role of Lamont Cranston. Seeing the handwriting on the wall, when the Shadow series was discontinued the handsome leading man took a job as sales representative for a national clothing manufacturer. He continued to act when he could, landing the title role in another serial based on a comic strip, *Brick Bradford* (1947), and taking his last part in *Stage Struck* (1948).

By coincidence, Richmond was walking down a Los Angeles street, on his way to a sales call with sample case in hand, when he passed a theater just as a showing of the latter ended and audience members filed out. He was instantly recognized and mobbed by picture fans demanding his autograph. Some of them were puzzled to see him carrying a sample case filled with clothes. Richmond found the whole situation humiliating and vowed on the spot to cut his ties with Hollywood forever. Many years later, relating the above story to *Screen Thrills Illustrated* co-editor Samuel M. Sherman, the silver screen's fourth Shadow remained bitter about his career and regarded his three films as the Master of Darkness with little affection.

The surprise cancellation in 1949 of *The Shadow Magazine* effectively removed—in the near term, at least—any hope of reviving the character in motion pictures. The Shadow radio show continued to air on Sunday afternoons over the Mutual network, with Bill Johnstone having been replaced by Bret Morrison in 1943. Movie actor John Archer, the father of actress Anne Archer, spelled Morrison for the 1944-45 season, after which Bret reclaimed the role and played it through the series finale in 1954.

That same year saw production of a half-hour Shadow TV pilot based entirely on the character's radio incarnation. An outfit called Meridian Pictures, owned by one John E. Gibbs, licensed limited television rights to the property from Street & Smith. Producers Nathan Kroll and Wilson Tuttle commissioned Peter Barry, whose credits included teleplays for such shows as *Studio One* and *Robert Montgomery Presents*, to write a script structured like a Shadow radio episode—something that could be shot quickly and cheaply on flimsy sets in a tiny Manhattan studio.

Titled "The Case of the Cotton Kimono," the pilot starred British actor Tom Helmore as Lamont Cranston. A fairly prolific screen performer in his native country during the Thirties, Helmore came to America during World War II and became a Broadway actor, flirting with Hollywood in the late Forties but returning to New York in 1950 to work on stage and in live TV. Helmore was a good chum of Boris Karloff, even after Tom's wife divorced him in 1945 and subsequently married the horror-film star. Handsome and mustached, he made a suitably urbane Cranston. Paula Raymond, a one-time M-G-M contract player since reduced to "B" pictures, had stayed in New York after finishing location work on *The Beast from 20,000 Fathoms* and was cast as Margot Lane. Veteran character actor Frank M. Thomas, another player who hopped from stage to screen, played Commissioner Weston.

Barry's script made Lamont Cranston a psychiatrist on retainer to the New York Police Department—a deviation from the radio program, but a sensible one. He's called in to help investigate the murder of a woman wearing a cotton kimono, and interrogates the chief suspects after visiting them privately as The Shadow. The culprit is revealed to be a corrupt detective who framed the victim's hapless boyfriend but couldn't fool Cranston. Director Charles Haas didn't waste any time trying to visualize the character: Helmore's Shadow, like the radio show's, was just an eerie, disembodied voice, enhanced with the same sort of milk-bottle effect heard by Mutual listeners. Raymond and Thomas were fine in their roles but the pilot's pedestrian storyline and threadbare production values doomed it from the beginning. Reportedly, the ad agency representing Pall Mall Cigarettes showed interest in the series but never followed through.

A second pilot was made in 1958 by New York-based producer Emanuel Demby; it appears to be the only filmed program with which he was involved. He obtained screen rights from Conde Nast, which had purchased the Street & Smith properties. Somehow Demby became involved with New Orleans-based producer Eric Sayers, whose only previous film was the sleazy crime thriller *New Orleans After Dark*. Apparently Sayers persuaded Demby to have the story based in the Big Easy and shot on location. To this end he recruited local director John Sledge, who had recently helmed two Nola-shot TV episodes as well as *After Dark*.

Prolific TV writer George Bellak penned the teleplay, which made Lamont Cranston a criminologist and gentleman adventurer. Absent were Margot, Weston, Shrevvy, and all vestiges of the radio show except Cranston's ability to cloud men's minds. According to Bellak, Lamont learned the secrets of the East from a mystic named Jogendra, who was not only his mentor but also his constant companion. The plot revolved around a democratically elected Latin American ruler deposed in a military coup and living in New Orleans pending the outcome of a planned revolt. A Betty Jeffries shared screen credit with Bellak, but as *Invisible Avenger* appears to be her only film one wonders how much she contributed to the script.

Perhaps the most mysterious aspect of this 1958 Shadow pilot was the involvement of Oscar-winning cinematographer James Wong Howe, somehow inveigled to co-direct with John Sledge. There's no documentary evidence linking him to any of the participants, although he may have befriended someone in the small, tight-knit New Orleans film community when he shot part of Jeff Chandler's Civil War drama *Drango* on location in nearby Fort Pike the previous year.

The 57-minute pilot, which had gone into production as *The Shadow*, failed to sell. Its optical effects and film processing had been done by

Invisible Avenger's one-sheet downplayed any connection to the Shadow of yore.

Hollywood's Consolidated Film Industries, a subsidiary of Herbert J. Yates' Republic Pictures Corporation. One might reasonably assume that Demby and Sayers owed money to Consolidated and agreed to let Republic distribute the busted pilot as a theatrical offering. Retitled *Invisible Avenger*, the hour-long film reached movie screens on December 2, 1958.

Various sources cite Republic as the production entity, although the film carries no copyright notice and its advertising materials refer to it as a Republic Presentation rather than a Republic Picture or Production. It stands to reason that Demby and Sayers produced the pilot under corporate auspices, if only to give themselves liability protection. Shadow scholar Martin Grams credits production to a Demby Productions, Inc., but no such company is mentioned either on screen or on *Avenger*'s posters.

Advertising and marketing aids pointedly omitted any tie-in with The Shadow of pulp or radio fame. Poster copy referred to "the unseen shadow man," which is as close as *Invisible Avenger* got to acknowledging its ostensible source material.

Invisible Avenger begins with a fixed view of a dark New Orleans street. A church bell tolls and an English-accented voice intones, "Who knows what evil lurks in the hearts of men? Only The Shadow knows!"

At a New Orleans nightclub Pablo Ramirez (Dan Mullin), deposed president of the Latin American country Santa Cruz, and his daughter Felicia (Jeanne Neher) ask jazz musician Tony Alcadé (Steve Dano) to enlist the aid of his friend, criminologist Lamont Cranston (Richard Derr). Ramirez has been in exile since his twin brother Victor engineered a military coup to overthrow Santa Cruz's democratic government. Pablo's loyal followers are preparing a revolt to be led by their ex-presidenté, but Ramirez is under observation by the dictator's spies, operating out of a New Orleans nightclub owned by Tara O'Neill (Helen Westcott).

Tony Alcadé phones Cranston at the latter's New York home but has only told Lamont half the story, barely mentioning Tara, when he is killed by her accomplice, Ramon "Rocco" Martinez (Leo Bruno). Rocco then reports to his superior, the Colonel (Lee Edwards), who instructs his underling to have one of their operatives, a cab driver named Charlie (Sam Page), meet Cranston when he flies into the airport.

Lamont is accompanied on his trip to New Orleans by his mentor Jogendra (Mark Daniels), who has taught him the ancient Eastern techniques of mesmerism and telepathy. Using his power to cloud men's minds, the American criminologist becomes a shadowy figure in the rear of Charlie's cab and befuddles the duplicitous driver. He wonders what became of his friend Tony. That night, keeping his appointment to meet Tara on a street corner. Jogendra, sensing danger, sends a telepathic warning to his pupil, enabling Lamont to narrowly avoid an onrushing truck meant to kill him "accidentally."

Cranston later sneaks into Tara's Bourbon Street club, discovers Tony's body hidden in a piano, and is attacked by Rocco, from whom he escapes. Once again becoming the invisible Shadow, he visits Pablo and Felicia; fearing for their lives, he directs the refugees to a new hiding place and urges them to call his friend Lamont Cranston should they require further assistance.

The next evening, a television news broadcast indicates that the turncoat, Victor Ramirez, is about to be executed for conspiring to overthrow the Generalissimo with whom he engineered Pablo's dethroning. With his last words, Victor begs his brother to forgive his betrayal and come out of hiding to lead Santa Cruz to freedom. Subsequently, Felicia phones Cranston to inform him that Pablo intends to honor his brother's dying wish. Lamont agrees to join Pablo the next day but soon becomes separated from the former presidenté, who is summarily kidnapped. Adopting the Shadow persona to investigate, Cranston learns that Pablo has been spirited away in a coffin and loaded onto a ship by the Colonel and his operatives.

Diverted to a cemetery, Lamont and Felicia realize they've been duped but manage to trace Pablo to the ship. They board the vessel and come face to face with the girl's uncle Victor, whose "execution" was a ruse staged to draw the deposed monarch out of hiding. Jogendra tricks the captain into cutting the ship's engines by making him believe an iceberg looms ahead. In the ensuing confusion, Lamont turns into The Shadow, clouding the minds of both Victor and the Colonel, who fatally shoot each other in the confusion. Their henchmen, having learned that the revolt has succeeded, lay down their arms. Once again a free man, Pablo makes plans to return to Santa Cruz and retake his throne. The film ends as it began, with that same view of the darkened New Orleans street and the repetition of The Shadow's famous tagline.

Invisible Avenger is rather an ignominious effort that does considerable violence to The Shadow's character. Richard Derr plays Lamont Cranston as an insouciant buttinski and something of a skirt-chaser. Mark Daniels as Jogendra is perhaps the least convincing Asian character in film history. In an early scene Pablo Ramirez refers to The Shadow with respect and awe, but at no time does Cranston's alter ego do anything to justify his reputation. The whole affair is depressingly pedestrian.

73

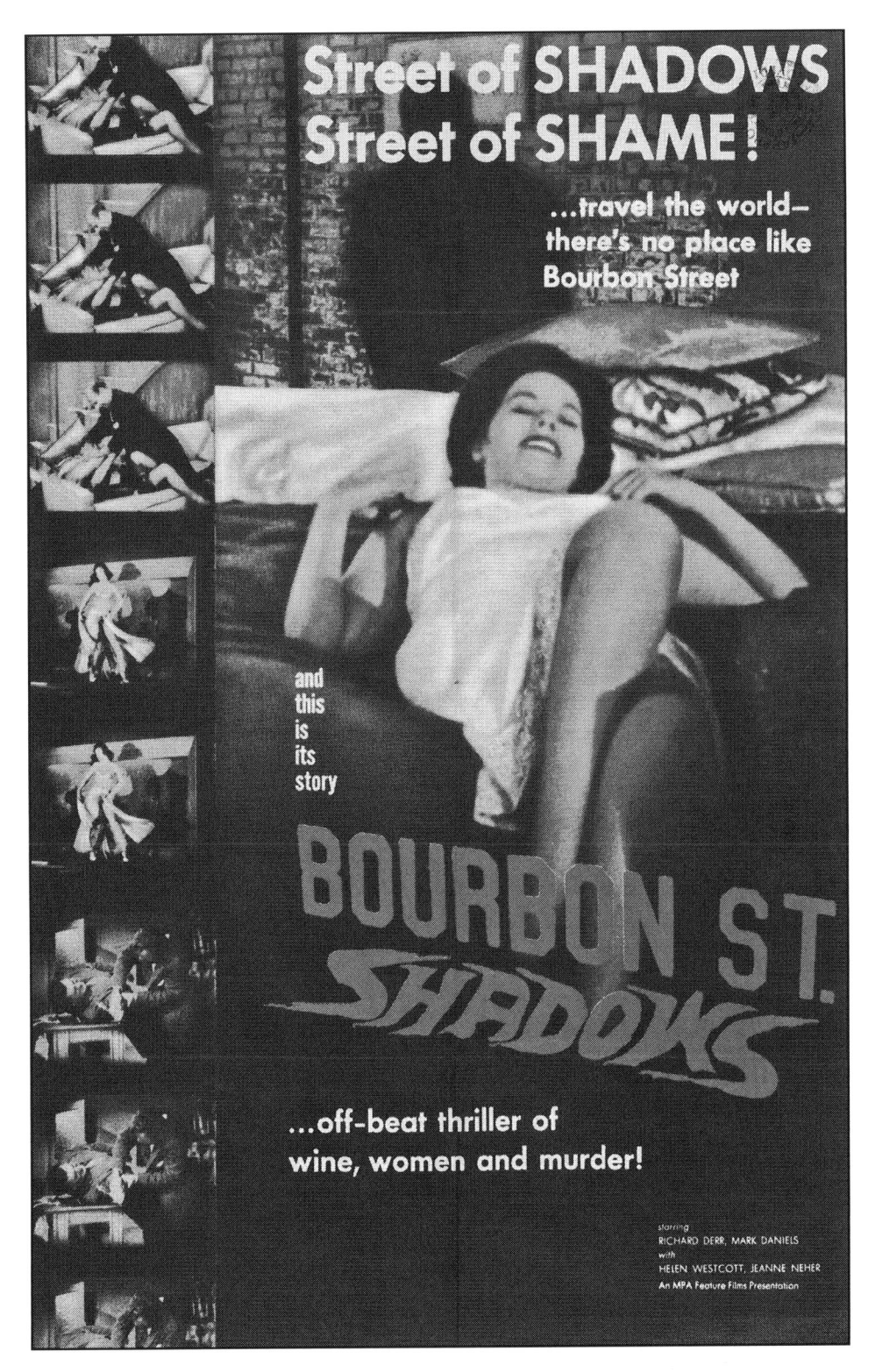

Production values are conspicuous by their absence, and while it's easy to tell that actual New Orleans locations (especially along Bourbon Street) are being lensed, very little is done to exploit the area's picturesque qualities. A sequence shot inside Lakefront Airport was dubbed for sound afterward, and none too convincingly.

The visuals are surprisingly mundane, especially given the pictorial expertise of co-director Howe. Most shots are framed perfunctorily which virtually no attempt at atmospheric lighting, clever angling, or dramatic camera movements. Joseph Wheeler's photography is competent but nothing more. In a throwback to the Monogram films, Howe and Sledge portray Lamont Cranston's other self as a disembodied shadow on the wall, and one not-terribly-well-executed closeup shows his silhouetted hand turning a television dial. But here, too, a lack of imagination and obviously rushed shooting defeat the filmmakers' intentions.

The motion-picture trade publications ignored *Invisible Avenger*; no contemporary reviews of the film have been found. It played in tandem with other Republic releases and made the rounds of theaters nationwide for nearly a year before being retired. In New York during early 1959, for example, the Shadow opus was the bottom half of a double bill top-lined by a feature version of the company's 1937 serial *Zorro Rides Again*, hastily cut down to capitalize on the success of Walt Disney's *Zorro* TV series. *Avenger* was occasionally paired with films released by other distributors.

By year's end the Republic Pictures Corporation had exited the theatrical market and had licensed its film library to National Telefilm Associates. As an independent production only released by Republic, *Invisible Avenger* was not included in that deal.

In 1962 Eric Sayers turned the Shadow film over to New Orleans director Ben Parker, who hired cinematographer Willis Winford to shoot additional scenes of a moderately sleazy nature, which were then added to *Invisible Avenger*. The resulting motion picture, only a few minutes longer than its predecessor, was titled *Bourbon St.* [sic] *Shadows* and given an exploitation campaign that didn't mention The Shadow (or even "the shadow man"). Released under the auspices of Louisiana-based MPA Feature Films, Inc., the retooled epic circulated mostly in the South and on the East Coast for another couple years before vanishing altogether. *Invisible Avenger*, having never been copyrighted, has been released on DVD by several distributors of public-domain movies and is available for viewing on the YouTube internet site, which also carries a coming-attractions trailer for *Bourbon St. Shadows*.

The Master of Darkness experienced a three-pronged revival in the early 1960s. Radio-industry veteran Charles Michelson in 1963 began syndicating a group of the Shadow radio programs, as well as episodes of such other favorites as *The Lone Ranger* and *The Green Hornet*. These old shows did surprisingly well and played in some major markets. That same year Walter B. Gibson wrote a paperback original, *Return of The Shadow*, published by Belmont Books; it was followed by a updated series of novels, with Dennis Lynds writing as Maxwell Grant, that made the title character a special agent along *Man from U.N.C.L.E* lines. Then, in 1964, Archie Comics launched a Shadow comic book that initially featured a blonde Lamont Cranston (!) wearing the familiar black cloak and battling his most persistent pulp-magazine adversary, Shiwan Khan. A catastrophic miscalculation had The Shadow soon turning into a costumed superhero wearing an ugly blue-and-green, long-underwear outfit. Mercifully, the lackluster comic was terminated after eight issues.

In the early 1970s a rumor circulated to the effect that TV's Lone Ranger, Clayton Moore, had late in the preceding decade starred in an unsold Shadow pilot inspired by the success of the Batman series. Old-Time-Radio aficionado Jim Harmon gave the rumor currency by repeating it in his 1992 book *Radio Mystery and Adventure*. However, Moore's daughter Dawn recently told me there is nothing to that speculation. A quarter decade would pass before Hollywood once again embraced the Master of Darkness.

When Shadow aficionados assemble and the conversation eventually turns to the 1994 film starring Alec Baldwin and Penelope Ann Miller, you're sure to hear a wide range of opinions. Some believe *The Shadow* to be wonderful, a lavishly mounted and exciting thriller that finally does justice to a hero previously victimized in cheap, unimaginative "B" pictures. Others believe it to be a desecration, a bafflingly brain-dead opus that disrespects both radio and pulp incarnations of the character. A third fan constituency—perhaps the largest—praises some aspects of the film while condemning others. Among members of this group, the consensus is that director Russell Mulcahy and screenwriter David Koepp got about as much wrong as they did right. After analyzing scripts commissioned from the three major writers assigned to the project over an eight-year period, we're here to tell you that, however flawed the 1994 *Shadow* may be, it could have been worse. A lot worse. But it could just as easily have been better. Much better.

By the time it was released in July of 1994, *The Shadow* had been in the works for more than 15 years. In 1978, merchandising agent Stan Weston's Leisure Concepts Inc. secured rights to the character from Condé

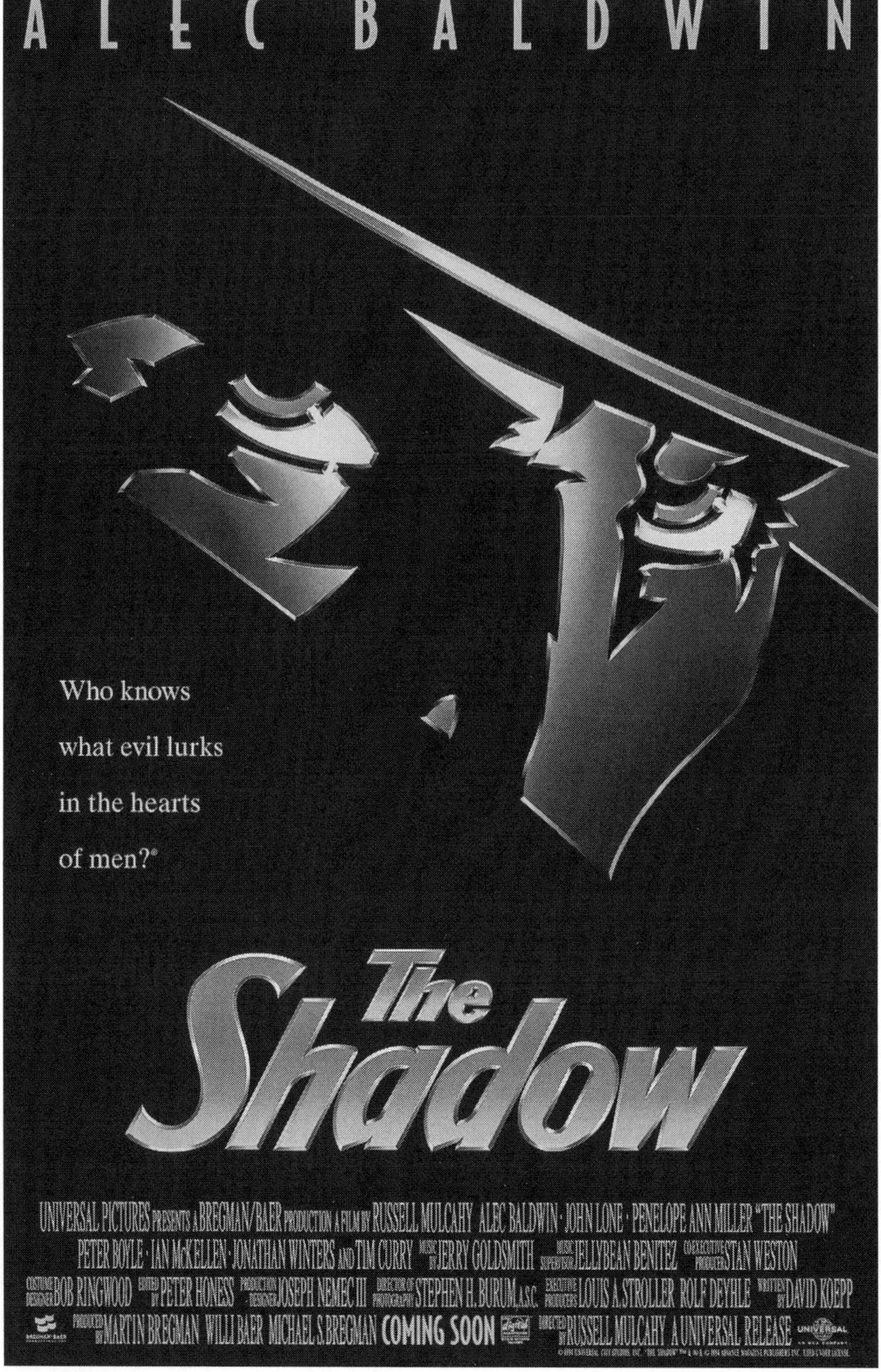
ALEC BALDWIN
Who knows what evil lurks in the hearts of men?
The Shadow
UNIVERSAL PICTURES PRESENTS A BREGMAN/BAER PRODUCTION A FILM BY RUSSELL MULCAHY ALEC BALDWIN · JOHN LONE · PENELOPE ANN MILLER "THE SHADOW"
PETER BOYLE · IAN McKELLEN · JONATHAN WINTERS AND TIM CURRY MUSIC BY JERRY GOLDSMITH MUSIC SUPERVISOR JELLYBEAN BENITEZ CO-EXECUTIVE PRODUCER STAN WESTON
COSTUME DESIGNER BOB RINGWOOD EDITED BY PETER HONESS PRODUCTION DESIGNER JOSEPH NEMEC III DIRECTOR OF PHOTOGRAPHY STEPHEN H. BURUM, A.S.C. EXECUTIVE PRODUCERS LOUIS A. STROLLER ROLF DEYHLE WRITTEN BY DAVID KOEPP
PRODUCED BY MARTIN BREGMAN WILLI BAER MICHAEL S. BREGMAN COMING SOON DIRECTED BY RUSSELL MULCAHY A UNIVERSAL RELEASE
UNIVERSAL

Nast Publications for $10,000 and an undisclosed partnership in all future Shadow revenue. Weston sold the film rights to Universal two and a half years later. *Variety* reported that the deal included a $250,000 advance to Leisure Concepts (a Conde Nast subsidiary), a role as executive producer with $100,000 bonus, and 20 percent of the film's profits.

The huge successes of *Superman II* (1980) and *Raiders of the Lost Ark* (1981) likely persuaded Universal executives to undertake development of a Shadow film. With big-budget "superhero" movies and decidedly retro action thrillers cleaning up at the nation's box offices, they probably figured a new take on a vintage crime buster might be just the thing to bring adventure-hungry audiences back into the theaters.

Gossip columns and the Hollywood trade papers gleefully printed speculative tidbits regarding possible directors and stars. Both Ben Cross (coming off the award-winning *Chariots of Fire*) and John Travolta (taken more seriously as a leading man after his performance in *Blow Out*) were mentioned as contenders for the title role.

Leslie Newman, who co-wrote the first two Salkind-produced Superman movies with her husband David, was commissioned to whip up a Shadow script, which she completed early in 1982. (By that time the property had been assigned to producer Martin Bregman for development.) It's not known how extensively Newman researched her subject, but she obviously read "The Shadow's Shadow," a 1933 novel reprinted in paperback as part of the Pyramid/Jove series of the mid '70s. From that story—an exceptionally good, early Shadow adventure—she took the villain, Felix Zubian, and one of his reminiscences about World War I, which she expanded into a credible back story.

Newman's script begins in 1917, with 25-year-old socialite Lamont Cranston (whom she describes as "lean and hawk-nosed, darkly handsome with intense, haunting eyes") mastering foreign languages and taking lessons in jiu jitsu, flying, and marksmanship. Independently wealthy but bored with the frivolous pastimes of his social set, Cranston hosts garden parties at his Long Island estate but takes no particular pleasure from them. At one such soiree he meets Margo Lane, a plucky, outspoken girl who climbs the ivy-covered wall to his balcony in an attempt to crash the party. Newman describes her as "very young, slender, awkward, and enchanting." The repartee that ensues is cleverly written and endearing, if somewhat out of character for an action-adventure film. It's apparent that Margo is instantly smitten with Cranston. "In one hour," writes Newman of their first meeting, "this 16-year-old tomboy has lost her heart for a lifetime."

The Shadow (Alec Baldwin) is seen for the first time in the classic bridge scene.

No long afterwards, Lamont Cranston volunteers to go overseas with the American Expeditionary Forces and becomes a master spy, putting to good use the various skills he has spent years developing. His counterpart is Baron Felix Zubian, "the pride of German intelligence," whom Cranston's commanding officer describes as having "genius, daring, all your skills—everything but a conscience."

Cranston routinely foils Zubian's plots, earning the undying enmity of the Kaiser's top spy. While on leave in Paris, Lamont meets and falls in love with French shopgirl Lucie Berthier, to whom he becomes engaged. Some time later, on the very day the Armistice is signed, the vengeful Zubian follows Cranston to Paris and accidentally kills Lucie with a bullet intended for the American. Broken-hearted and unaware that Zubian was the assassin, Lamont returns to America and hurls himself into the full-time study of occult sciences.

Five years pass. Zubian, accompanied by his chief aide Gromek, comes to the United States to pursue a life of crime. Posing as a Frenchman, the Marquis de Favreaux, he manages to obtain an estate on Long Island not far from the Cranston family homestead. At a get-acquainted party thrown by his new neighbor, Lamont runs into Margo. "At 22," writes Newman, "she is no longer gawky, just magnificently coltish and as bright as she is beautiful." (Throughout the script, Newman's treatment of The Shadow's

Commissioner Barth (Jonathan Winters, left) and Lamont Cranston (Alec Baldwin).

faithful friend and companion indicates that she finds Margo a far more interesting character than the Master of Darkness.)

Zubian has a good reason for staging his lavish party: By gathering together his wealthy neighbors, he leaves their homes empty and fair game for the larcenous Gromek and his henchmen. A million-dollar jewel robbery, pulled off that very night, results in the implication of a servant whom Lamont clears by breaking into the home to prove the lad incapable of having carried out the theft. Garbed in black hat and cloak, he is seen by the mistress of the house, who later describes him to police as "a shadowy apparition." A subsequent newspaper headline, "Drake Estate Robbed Again By 'Shadow,'" gives our hero the name by which he will be forevermore known.

It's taken Newman 45 script pages to get to this point, and she wastes another 30 on a superfluous subplot involving an offshore gambling ship and white slavers. This lengthy sequence, which culminates in The Shadow's rescue of the women imprisoned on board the ship, establishes a connection between Zubian and local gang leader Floyd Flynn (a big investor in the floating casino), but otherwise adds little to the story. It does, however, give Margo something else to do, which is clearly one of Newman's priorities.

Harry Vincent, who in the pulps was one of The Shadow's most capable agents, turns up on the gambling ship as a nervous waiter. An ex-con who's had trouble finding work, he later agrees reluctantly to act as

Margo Lane (Penelope Ann Miller) meets Lamont initially at the Cobalt Club.

getaway driver on one of Gromek's jewel heists, which ends in a murder. Captured and confronted by The Shadow, Harry makes amends by acting as bait in a trap that ensnares Gromek and results in the death of Zubian's long-time aide.

With The Shadow's net closing in on him, the "Marquis" resorts to desperate measures. At this point, with the movie drawing to a close, Newman loses her way altogether. What's supposed to be an exciting climactic sequence—the kidnapping and attempted murder of Lamont and Margo by Flynn's henchmen—falls flat. Flynn evades capture altogether, an unusual lapse for a film like this one.

Zubian finally resolves to kill Cranston. (By this time Lamont, for his part, has discovered that the Marquis is not only Zubian, but also the killer of his fiancée.) He slips into the Cranston home one night and, entering the bedroom, fires point blank into the figure huddled under the covers. At this point The Shadow slips out from behind a drape and disarms the surprised villain. Turns out it was Margo under the covers, wearing a bulletproof vest under Lamont's pajamas.

Cranston, you see, anticipated the attack. As he's being dragged off to jail, Felix Zubian blurts out, "But I don't understand. Where is Lamont Cranston?" To which Margo replies, "The Shadow knows." Fade out. The End. Predictably, Newman has given *her* the final word, not Lamont Cranston.

Shiwan Khan (John Lone), like his illustrious ancestor, plans to conquer the world.

This singularly lame denouement is perhaps the most egregious of the many flaws in Newman's screenplay. It's clear she had no feeling at all for The Shadow, no appreciation of the character's special traits and mythic status. In her view he's not the imposing figure of eerie mystery imagined by Walter Gibson, just another adventurer in a cape. Newman brought the sensibilities of the Superman scripts to her screenplay for The Shadow: to her, the core of the story is the Cranston-Lane interaction. The Shadow, like Superman, is simply a persona that prevents the male and female leads from having a normal relationship. To Newman, the venerable crime buster's heroics are almost incidental.

Newman's script was summarily dismissed and interest in the project flagged until 1985, when the names of Robert Zemeckis and Bob Gale—the team responsible for Universal's recent megahit, *Back to the Future*—were attached to *The Shadow*. Presumably it was Zemeckis, also the director of *Romancing the Stone*, who commissioned a screenplay from Howard Franklin, who made uncredited script contributions to that Michael Douglas-Kathleen Turner smash. Franklin submitted his first draft in May of 1986.

This new opus, also titled *The Shadow*, begins promisingly. The story opens, as per the date on a newspaper seen in the first shot, on March 28, 1938. A debutante has been kidnapped and buried alive to induce her wealthy father to pay the ransom quickly and without police interference.

81

Dr. Reinhardt Lane (Ian McKellen) and his assistant Farley Claymore (Tim Curry).

One of the kidnappers seizes the ransom money and disappears into the sewers beneath Manhattan. We see him scurrying through underground tunnels, finally emerging on a subway platform. He has been followed by a shadow that eventually addresses him in a "chilling, disembodied voice—mocking yet cultivated."

The thug is seized by invisible hands and held aloft; he can see his assailant's shadow on the tiled wall behind them. The Shadow, who has clouded this man's mind, relaxes his mental control long enough to become partially visible. He still holds the prisoner, who sees beneath the slouch hat a leering death's-head visage. Terrified, the kidnapper reels back and falls off the platform directly in the path of an oncoming train. Fortunately, he has told The Shadow where the girl was hidden, and she is rescued by a police task force accompanied by Commissioner Weston.

The Shadow returns to the Cranston home, identified in the script as a brownstone on East 64th Street. Exhausted, he removes hat and cloak and staggers into his bathroom. The figure he sees in the mirror is "still half-Shadow: his skin pale, his face taut, his eyes burning with intensity."

Once again Lamont Cranston, he retires to a "secret library" meant to substitute for the sanctum described by Gibson in the pulp stories. The library is littered with skulls and other artifacts, its walls lined with ancient volumes devoted to occult lore and Eastern mysticism. There he is joined by

Two Shadow agents: Moe Shrevnitz (Peter Boyle) and Dr. Roy Tam (Sab Shimono).

Margo Lane, "an attractive young woman with an earthy glamour, but one who 'has a past.' " That's true enough. This isn't any Margo we've heard in radio shows or read about in pulps and comics. She's a bit coarse, prone to dropping her g's and spouting mild profanity. Practically the first words she utters, upon being startled by Cranston, are: "For Chrissakes, Lamont!"

We learn that Margo is a former gun moll, the ex-mistress of gangster Dutch Deegan, who is to be executed that very night. She ratted him out after meeting, and subsequently falling in love with, Lamont Cranston. She alone knows that Cranston is The Shadow.

Dutch escapes the electric chair by hypnotizing the warden and various death-house guards, and with the aid of his henchmen—who've obviously been preparing for this night—he makes a daring escape from the prison. Deegan rushes back to his hideout (an abandoned warehouse bearing a sign that reads, "Walter Gibson & Sons—Grain & Feed") and eagerly embraces the one woman who remains loyal to him: his blind mother.

Almost immediately, and without explaining how he acquired the remarkable ability that enabled him to cheat the executioner, he begs Ma Deegan to tell him again how, pregnant and penniless, she was abandoned by her erstwhile lover, a man named James Lewis, who broke up with her at midnight on April Fool's Day, 1908, atop the old Waldorf-Astoria Hotel. This oft-repeated story obviously has great significance for Dutch.

Margot worries that her eccentric father is working too hard and liable to crack.

Franklin gradually unveils his Big Caper, a ludicrous scheme by Dutch to round up every James Lewis in Manhattan and herd them all into the Empire State Building, which replaced the old Waldorf-Astoria, on April Fool's Day. The gangster expects to hypnotize the men, bring them up to the observation platform, and command them to jump to their deaths at midnight. In this way, he reasons, the man who abandoned his mother is sure to meet a suitably horrible end, exactly 30 years after saying goodbye to Ma. That dozens of innocent men will also be killed is something that doesn't trouble Dutch in the least.

The absurdity of this plan is matched only by the revelation that Deegan, while imprisoned, read enough books to learn the secrets of hypnosis, mesmerism, and even the ancient Tibetan ritual by which The Shadow clouds men's minds to make himself invisible. Leaving aside the question of whether prison libraries would stock such tomes, it's awfully difficult to believe that a marginally literate thug would possess the discipline necessary to master such exacting skills. Franklin gets around this by having Dutch refer to all those months he spent in solitary confinement: The "alone time" enabled him to sharpen his concentration.

Unaware of Deegan's scheme, Cranston persuades Margo to return to her old gangland haunts—in other words, act as bait to draw out her former boyfriend. Initially Dutch is taken in by her, although Ma Deegan protests vigorously, telling her son that Margo betrayed him once and will

Khan becomes increasingly frustrated with Claymore's continued bungling.

likely do it again. Margo winds up hypnotized and brought to the Empire State Building on April Fool's Day night with some two-dozen men named James Lewis.

The Shadow arrives just a second before midnight and, in the ensuing battle of wills, unnerves the gangster by telling him the truth: His sweet old Ma was a notorious prostitute. In fact, says The Shadow, she slept with hundreds of men. "That's a lie!" Ma blurts out. "It was only 30, 40 men at the most." Sadly, this is cold comfort to Dutch, who takes a header off the observation deck as the Master of Darkness mops up the remaining opposition and breaks the hypnotic spells that have a couple dozen innocents—and Margo—perched on the edge of oblivion.

This script is a near-total miss, despite its atmospheric, potentially thrilling first sequence. Where Leslie Newman idealized the Cranston-Lane relationship, Franklin debases it by making Margo a borderline vulgarian. The low point is a scene in which a seriously injured, comatose, bedridden Lamont suddenly revives as Margo hovers over him. He kisses her savagely and "with the same sudden passion . . . puts his other hand hard against her thigh, kneads the flesh lasciviously, cups her buttock, flips himself over on top of her. He kisses her throat, her neck, begins to tear at her dress to get to her breasts."

The notion that Lamont's sexual assault on Margo represents an acceptable development is mind-boggling enough, but Franklin's excuse for

Margo is hypnotized by Khan into making a midnight attempt on Cranston's life.

it is risible in the extreme. According to the script, Lamont sheepishly subsides and explains his bizarre behavior thusly: "I'd put myself into a healing trance. I was subject to The Shadow's—inhuman intensity."

Besides the opening, the only worthwhile sequence in Franklin's screenplay is one in which The Shadow, to let Dutch know he can't escape detection forever, communicates with the gangster via the airwaves. Learning that Deegan's favorite dramatic program is the "Mystery Hour," he enters the radio station while invisible and frightens cast members and sound-effects men into leaving the studio. Then, playing a record of "Saint-Saens' Opus #31" (which was the theme of the Shadow radio show), he intones into the still-live microphone his legendary invocation: "Who knows what evil lurks in the hearts of men? The Shadow knows!" This is accompanied by a montage of people across the city— including families with children, huddled around their console radios—listening, wide-eyed and with mouths agape, to the chilling voice that warns: "Crime does not pay!"

Zemeckis and Gale moved on to other projects, including the *Back to the Future* sequels, and *The Shadow* languished in Development Hell for several more years. From time to time other names were associated with the property; at one time Sam Raimi was said to be interested in directing, and even the great Steven Spielberg supposedly considered doing the film. But nothing came of these reports. Finally, in 1990, newly minted screenwriter

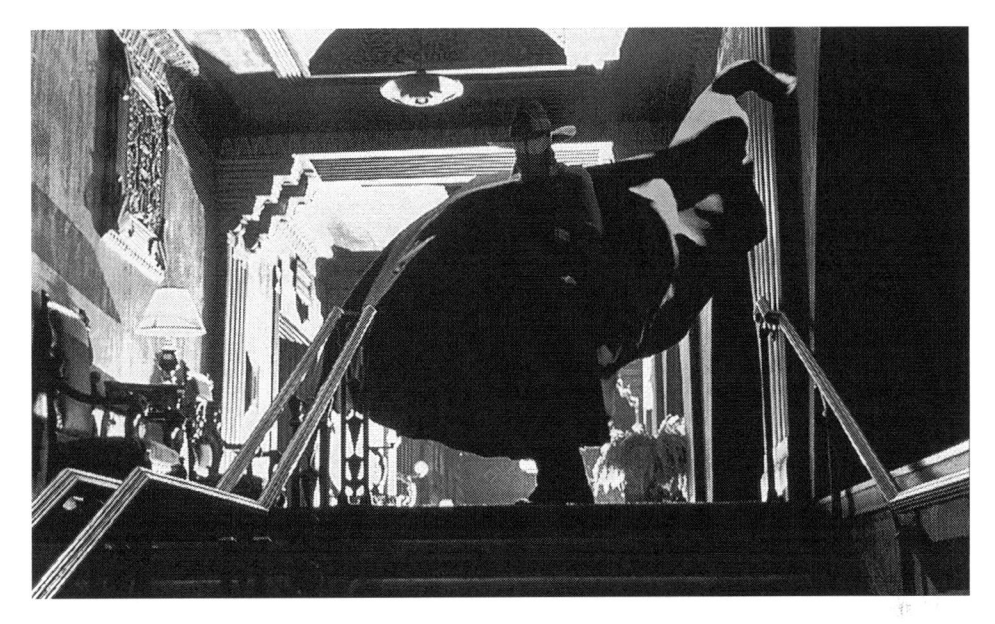

Having learned that Khan's headquarters is the old Hotel Monolith, The Shadow takes the fight to his adversaries by penetrating the Monolith's defenses at night.

David Koepp was commissioned to make his own pass at the property. His first script, dated June 12, was the basis for what became the 1994 film. Shadow fans today can only wish it had been shot as written.

Most of the movie's annoying facets—the "morphing" of Alec Baldwin's Lamont Cranston into the hawk-nosed avenger of George Rozen's classic pulp covers, some of the campy dialogue (including Khan and Cranston trading quips about haberdashery), the over-the-top comedic heavy played by Tim Curry, and most of all the "origin" sequence depicting Cranston as a ruthless drug lord—are absent from Koepp's initial draft, which stays relatively close to the pulps in both spirit and detail.

The first Koepp script includes Commissioner Weston rather than the lesser-known Wainwright Barth, and his relationship with Cranston mirrors that related in the novels and radio episodes. (The curious substitution of Barth in a later draft made that new Commissioner an exasperated uncle to irresponsible playboy Cranston, a throwback to George Callahan's scripts for the three 1946 Shadow movies produced by Monogram.) Koepp's earliest version of the famous bridge sequence, arguably the most satisfying in the entire movie, already includes references to "Diamond Bert" and "English Johnny," criminals who faced The Shadow in the first novel. What's more, The Shadow's autogiro, which appeared in many of the pulp yarns, figures prominently in the finale.

The Shadow vanquishes Claymore and Khan's Mongol Warriors in the Monolith.

Cabbie Moe Shrevnitz (played by Peter Boyle in the film) has a great deal more to do in Koepp's first draft. He, Margo, and recently recruited agent Roy Tam invade the Monolith Hotel from beneath while The Shadow does battle with Shiwan Khan. In fact, Koepp at one point has Shrevnitz wielding a tommy-gun and mowing down a row of Khan's warriors. Margo and the agents thus play a major role in the climax, rather than simply waiting outside the newly visible hotel. The final struggle between the Golden Master and the Master of Darkness has Khan attempting to escape in an autogiro with The Shadow dangling from its side while trying to seize control of the aircraft. Had it been used, this sequence would have supplied a considerably more exciting (if more expensive and difficult to shoot) finale to the film.

Alas, producer Martin Bregman adhered to the time-honored Hollywood tradition of rejecting a first-draft script on general principles. Presumably it was Bregman who insisted on numerous revisions—no less than seven of them, the last completed in January 1994, with the movie already in production.

In crafting his script Koepp kept in mind the radio Shadow's signature line, "Who knows what evil lurks in the hearts of men? The Shadow knows!" While working, the screenwriter wondered how The Shadow came to possess such knowledge. "I decided that perhaps it was because he was

Cranston's climactic struggle with Khan ends with a mammoth battle of wills.

uncomfortably familiar with the evil in his own heart," Koepp explained in an article for *Moviemaker*. He elected to make Shiwan Khan, a Gibson creation, the villain of the piece because "he was bold and he knew what he was doing—he wanted to conquer the world. That was very simple, maybe a little ambitious, but he knew exactly what he wanted." The Shadow's struggle against Khan, then, became what the scripter called "a story of guilt and atonement," because in the process of defeating this would-be conqueror the Master of Darkness was forced to confront his own demons.

The final-draft story begins in the Orient during the years following the first World War. A bored, cynical American named Lamont Cranston (Alec Baldwin) has migrated eastward and set himself up as an opium dealer and merciless warlord known as Ying Ko. Abducted by servants of the Tulku, a Tibetan holy man and master of occult sciences, Cranston is forcibly reformed and trained to fight evil as a means of expunging his sins. He learns how to "cloud men's minds" so that they cannot see his corporeal form; all that remains is his shadow. Returning to his native New York City, Cranston resumes his pre-war life as an indolent playboy but secretly fights crime as The Shadow. In this guise he rescues Dr. Roy Tam (Sab Shimono) from mobsters and recruits the Chinese medico into his corps of agents, among them the invaluable Moe Shrevnitz (Peter Boyle), whose private cab is always at The Shadow's service.

Cranston's Uncle Wainwright (Jonathan Winters), who serves as New York's Police Commissioner, is having dinner with his scapegrace nephew at a glamorous nightclub when they are approached by dazzling socialite Margo Lane (Penelope Ann Miller), whom the Commissioner considers a pest. She wants his department to help protect her father, eccentric inventor Reinhardt Lane (Ian McKellen), who is working on a top-secret project for the War Department. Lamont attempts to get away from Margo by using his psychic abilities, but the socialite has natural telepathic powers and resists the mental suggestion he attempts to plant in her mind.

The Shadow fears for the girl's father, and with good reason: Lane has fallen under a hypnotic spell created by Shiwan Khan (John Lone), last descendant of Genghis Khan and would-be conqueror of the world. He plans to fulfill his ancestor's goal of world domination. Khan too has studied under the Tulku, even mastering the fabled Phurba dagger, an enchanted weapon that reacts to targeted psychic commands.

Having been smuggled into the country via an ancient sarcophagus delivered to a New York museum, Khan contacts Cranston and tries to enlist his aid in the belief that the former Ying Ko has carries a thirst for blood in his heart. Following the brief confrontation that serves as his answer, Cranston brings a souvenir of the meeting—an eons-old Chinese chain—to Dr. Tam's laboratory for analysis. There he learns that the metal is bronzium, a less-pure form of uranium that can be used in an atomic bomb. Margo's father has been developing a beryllium sphere in which such a reaction can be generated. His disappearance persuades Cranston that Khan is close to perfecting the devastating weapon.

Subsequently, Khan hypnotizes Margo and sends her to assassinate the erstwhile Ying Ko, believing that Cranston will be forced to kill her and thus surrender once more to his dark side. The playboy narrowly escapes death at Margo's hands but at the cost of revealing his true self to the girl. He also survives an attempt on his life by Reinhardt's former assistant, Farley Claymore (Tim Curry), who has joined Shiwan Khan.

Ultimately Cranston learns that Khan's base of operations in the old Hotel Monolith, supposedly demolished long ago but still standing in what appears to be a vacant lot. By using his own powers The Shadow sees through the mind-clouding haze in which his adversary has shrouded the hotel. Entering the Monolith, he battles Khan's Mongol warriors and terrifies Claymore into jumping through a window to his death far below. In a last desperate struggle with the conqueror, The Shadow nearly falls victim to the Phurba but manages to wrest mental control of it from Khan. Upon being

The decision to make Alec Baldwin's face conform to the pulp magazine's image of The Shadow required the handsome actor to undergo a rigorous makeup process that not only took up valuable time but also had grotesque results. It was both laborious and unneccessary: Since The Shadow habitually clouded the minds of his adversaries, who would even *know* about his hawk nose and piercing eyes? It was one of numerous miscalculations that harmed the movies, especially since the vast majority of moviegoers would be unfamiliar with the character's distinctive look.

wounded by the dagger, Shiwan loses his concentration and the Monolith suddenly becomes visible to New Yorkers passing by. He also involuntarily relinquishes hypnotic control of Lane, who with Margot's assistance manages to stop the planned explosion with seconds to spare.

Face to face with Khan in a mirrored room, The Shadow uses his mind's power to shatter the glass and launch a shard into the villain's brain. Shiwan's life is saved by a lobotomy that removes the part of the brain housing his psychic abilities, but he is locked in a padded room in a mental hospital overseen by one of The Shadow's agents. This leaves the Master of Darkness free to continue his war against evil.

Koepp's unnecessary and questionable back-story rather spectacularly differed from Walter Gibson's version of The Shadow's origin, yet the screenwriter clearly did his homework. It's evident he read all four Shiwan Khan novels, scenes and images from which were sprinkled throughout the script. To wit:

Professor Lane's hypnosis via cigarette-advertising billboard was inspired by a similar scene in "The Golden Master" that found proxy hero Paul Brent mesmerized by an electric sign outside his hotel-room window. In the same story, trusted agent Harry Vincent fell under Khan's hypnotic control and was sent to assassinate The Shadow. Koepp assigned this duty to Margo. The second novel in the quartet, "Shiwan Khan Returns," had even more influence on the screenwriter. From it he borrowed the concepts of the beryllium sphere (it's actually a bathysphere in Gibson's yarn) and Khan using the long-abandoned Hotel Monolith as his headquarters. Koepp also appropriated from "Returns" a striking visual effect cleverly realized on screen: The Shadow briefly immobilized by a thrown spear that pierces his cloak and pins him to a wall until he tears free.

The movie made much ado about an enchanted dagger called "the Phurba," which seemed to have a life of its own. This particular story device was culled from "The Invincible Shiwan Khan," third of the four Golden Master novels. Additionally, Dr. Roy Tam, The Shadow's chief Chinatown agent, played a substantial role in this story, which may account for this seldom-used character's prominence in Koepp's screenplay. "Masters of Death," last and arguably best installment of the Shiwan Khan saga, opened with the super-villain being smuggled into America inside the silver coffin of his ancestor, Genghis Khan. Koepp incorporated this event as well as Gibson's reference to Marpa Tulku, a Tibetan mystic who uses his occult powers to aid The Shadow.

(The scripter relied heavily on Gibson's novels but also included a nod to the Shadow radio show by setting a scene in the Temple of the Cobra, a reference to "The Temple Bells of Neban," the fifth episode in the 1937-38 season starring Orson Welles.)

Some fans have allotted Koepp the lion's share of blame for the movie's flaws, but it turns out that he, in the first draft, came closest of anybody to penning a satisfactory adaptation that combined the best features of both radio show and pulp series. Certainly he did a better job than either Newman or Franklin. Koepp can, however, be faulted for letting Alec Baldwin's snarky sense of humor infiltrate Lamont Cranston; he later admitted to incorporating some of Baldwin's wisecracks into the script.

Principal photography of *The Shadow* began on September 27, 1993 and consumed more than 60 working days, ending on January 28, 1994. Most of the film was staged and photographed on the Universal lot, with lavishly appointed sets sprawling across five soundstages. The famous Ambassador Hotel, located on Wilshire Boulevard in Los Angeles, was pressed into service, as was Pasadena's picturesque Mayfield Senior School. Sequences taking place in China were shot over a period of several days in the Alabama Hills adjoining Lone Pine, a small town nestled at the foot of the Sierra Nevada Mountains.

The Shadow's action climax, staged in a "house of mirrors" as a homage to the 1948 Orson Welles thriller, *The Lady from Shanghai*, was scaled back dramatically owing to an unpredictable natural disaster: On January 17, southern California was hit hard by the Northridge Earthquake, which registered a whopping 6.7 on the Richter Scale and caused an estimated $20 billion in damage. The quake shattered mirrors purchased for the movie's climactic face-off, and with time and money in equally short supply, Bregman's production team was forced to stage the sequence on a smaller scale than planned.

The film was originally budgeted at $25 million, but according to some reports its final cost ballooned to nearly $40 million. Releasing the movie in July, Universal clearly intended *The Shadow* to be a summer blockbuster but failed to market it effectively. During the early part of the playoff period it was outperformed at the nation's box offices by Disney's *The Lion King*, and during the later period by Jim Carrey's breakout feature, *The Mask*. The opening-weekend take was approximately $11,700,000, and the domestic gross topped out at $32,055,248. International ticket sales brought the worldwide total to approximately $48 million, but Universal's expenditures on prints and advertising were not recouped and the film was considered a flop. It did, however, perform extremely well in the prerecorded-video market, first on VHS and then on laserdisc. Sales were so strong that the studio briefly considered producing a direct-to-video sequel, and when Universal entered the DVD market in 1997 *The Shadow* was among four titles that constituted its initial release slate for the new format. There's no question that the movie has drawn and held a significant following. But whether Hollywood is ever able to improve upon it—or whether it even wants to—remains an unanswered question. And if The Shadow knows, he's not talking.

Printed in Great Britain
by Amazon